BREAKING BALLS

To Helmut Sundermann

'A kinder gentleman treads not the earth.'

William Shakespeare, *The Merchant of Venice*

John Scally

Breaking Balls

THE FUNNY SIDE OF THE GAA

CURRACH
·PRESS·

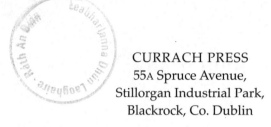

CURRACH PRESS
55A Spruce Avenue,
Stillorgan Industrial Park,
Blackrock, Co. Dublin

First published 2013
This edition, revised and updated, 2014

Cover design by sin é design
Origination by Currach Press
Printed by Bell & Bain Ltd

ISBN 978 1 78218 839 1

Contents

Acknowledgements

This book has been over twenty years in the making and draws heavily on interviews with many of the greats of both football and hurling who I have had the good fortune to meet. This includes some who have passed on to their eternal reward such as Dermot Earley, Mick Dunne, Jack Lynch, Seán Purcell, Dermot O'Brien, John B. Keane, Tim Kennelly, John Wilson, Jimmy Murray, Tom McNicholas and Eamonn Coleman to name just a few.

While this book was being written I was hugely saddened by the death of the legendary Páidí Ó Sé and the first chapter is a tribute to the great man. Likewise I will miss Clare legend Jimmy Smyth who is also featured among these pages. A heavy cloud of sadness fell on me with the news of the death of Seán Freyne, Mayo's most fanatical fan. Goodbye to you my trusted friend.

I could have never have constructed a work like this without the expert guidance of:

Mick Bermingham, Jimmy Barry-Murphy, Seán Boylan, Nickey Brennan, Seamus Bonner, Francie Brolly, Joe Brolly, DJ Carey, Martin Carney, Tom Carr, Brian Carthy, John Connolly, Matt Connor, Brian Corcorcan, Anthony Daly, Declan Darcy, Jimmy Deenihan, Joe Dunphy, Dermot Earley, Paul Earley, Nicky English, Dermot Flanagan, Jim Fives, Ciaran Fitzgerald, Jimmy Flynn, Mick Galwey, Seamus Hayden, Nudie Hughes, Babs Keating, Harry Keegan, Eddie Keher, Brendan Kennelly, Enda Kenny, TJ Kilgallon, Noel Lane, Pat Lindsay, Brian Lohan, Ger Loughnane, Brendan Lynch, Packy McGarty, Eugene McGee, Willie McGee, Peter McGinnity, Jim McKeever, John McKnight, Máirín

McAleenan, Seánie McMahon, Tony McManus, Enda McNulty, Kevin McStay, Jimmy Magee, Tim Maher, Pat Mangan, John Maughan, Barnes Murphy, Danny Murray, Jamesie O'Connor, Gay O'Driscoll, Mick O'Dwyer, Eamonn O'Hara, John O'Mahony, Micheál Ó Muircheartaigh, Colm O'Rourke, Kevin O'Neill, Mary O'Neill, John Purcell, Brian Talty, Paddy Prendergast, Martin Quigley, Paddy Quirke, Billy Quinn, Sue Ramsbottom, Gay Sheeran, Donie Shine and Kevin Walsh.

There are many more, too many to name individually, but I am thankful for all their insights. As always I am very grateful to Peter Woods for sharing his passion for the GAA with me.

Thanks to my good friend John Tiernan for his supply of amusing GAA stories.

Special thanks to the one and only Pat Spillane, who provided me with so many funny stories down through the years.

Sporting legend Tony Ward was much in my thoughts while this book was being written and his friendship will always be highly prized.

My particular gratitude to Paul Earley for his practical support and his own supply of funny stories.

The sporting event not of the year, if not of the decade, but of the century, if not the millennium, was St Brigid's historic All-Ireland senior club football triumph on St Patrick's Day. The icing on the cake was that the man of the match was Karol Mannion. Karol had his own match of the day that Christmas when he married Emir. Best wishes to both for a lifetime of happiness.

Thanks to Patrick, Michael and all at Currach Press for their help.

The Throw-In

A prominent GAA personality was driving home one night having drank a glass of lemonade too many and crashed into another vehicle. He was irate when a member of the Gardaí told him he was in trouble and said: 'Do you know who I am? I will have this sorted out within the hour.' He promptly texted the Taoiseach Enda Kenny and wrote: 'Enda, I'm in a bit of bother here and need your help. Ring me as soon as you can.' The only problem was that he mixed up the numbers and texted the Roscommon footballer Enda Kenny!

Although Eamon Dunphy claims 'rugby is the new sex', in the GAA world the truth is stranger than fiction and often funnier. From the beginning the GAA has had a history of abrasive characters, with the gift of rubbing people up the wrong way. Michael Cusack will always be remembered for his role in founding the GAA in 1884. Yet, having given birth to the Association, Cusack almost strangled it in his infancy, because of his abrasive personality. People often miss out on the historical significance of the 'Athletic' in the title of the GAA. In the early years it was envisaged that athletics would play a much greater role in the life of the GAA. One of the people trying to ensure this was John L. Dunbar. He wrote to Cusack in December 1885 suggesting that the GAA and the athletics organisation should meet 'with a view to a possible merger'. Cusack did not mince or waste his words in his response. The letter read as follows:

GAA
4 Gardiners Place
Dublin

Dear Sir,

I received your letter this morning and burned it.

Yours faithfully,
Michael Cusack

The great bard wrote: 'There is nothing so common as the wish to be remarkable.' Sadly I never made any real impact on GAA pitches. The former Dunfermline player Jim Leishman said: 'I was the first professional football player to be forced to retire due to public demand.' I had been the first amateur one in that very same situation. When I played underage for St Brigid's, All-Ireland senior club champions in 2013, the only real argument was over the most suitable nickname for my goalkeeping skills: Cinderella because I kept missing the ball, or Dracula because I was terrified of crosses.

Appropriately enough my football career began in a graveyard. An under-12 club match in Knockcrockery marked my initiation to championship football. There was no dressing room available at that time so we 'togged out' in a graveyard. It was so cold that I thought I discovered God's frozen people. It was to prove a metaphor for my career. My opponent was not the quickest. The milk in our kitchen turns faster. Although I never let him get a touch of the ball I was substituted at half-time. I never recovered from the injustice or the ignominy. Okay, so we were getting hammered but it wasn't my fault. It was obviously a political decision. What can a right full-back do when you can't even get close to the ball?

As my football career floundered my kind cousin decided to open another sporting career for me. He always claimed that I 'had a good eye' and on that basis decided I would be good at shooting. As he was accomplished marksman I trusted him implicitly. A Sunday afternoon was chosen for my investiture in my uncle's farmyard. An empty Bachelors peas tin was put up on the wall and I was instructed on how to take aim. I squeezed the trigger and nearly fell over with the 'kick' from the rifle. I looked up but the Bachelors peas tin was still gloriously intact. I could tell from the horror on my cousin's face that something terrible had happened. At first I couldn't find the problem but after a minute or two my eyes turned to the clothes line, about twenty yards away from the wall. There was now a big, gaping hole in my uncle's best shirt. Little wonder that my uncle has been shirty with me since. I never put my hand near a gun again.

My 'career' only really took off when I joined the ranks of the armchair fans. Some time later I drifted into sports writing. Again things didn't really go to plan. One of my first books was reviewed in the *Irish Times*. It should have been one of the great moments of my life but I was bemused to discover that I had a name change and that I was now 'Jean Scally'. I wrote a little note to the book's editor, John Banville, and informed him, 'Reports of my sex change have been greatly exaggerated.'

At times like this it is almost expected to talk about a labour of love. In my experience writing a book creates an awful lot of labour but very little love. A writer friend of James Joyce was dying after a traffic accident and someone insensitively asked him what dying was like and the writer with his final breath said, 'Oh Seánie its terrible but at least it's not nearly as bad as writing a book.'

Bill Shankly famously said, 'Some people believe football is a matter of life and death, I am very disappointed with that attitude. I can assure you it is much, much more important than that.' In professional sport today and increasingly at amateur level the desire to win is the dominant force. Sometimes it seems that we've taken the sport out of sporting activity. In a small way this book attempts to act as a corrective to that tendency. It strives simply to celebrate the fun that is attached to gaelic games and to give people a laugh or two.

Some people get totally out of shape when they retire from playing sport. Not so me. I was never in good shape in the first place. I took up running for a while but the closest I got to a marathon was to eat one of them – actually thousands of them.

However, I am part of a chosen few. There are four types of people: happy people, sad people, very sad people and then people who collect funny sports quotations and stories. I belong to that endangered species. My doctor agrees with this and has clinically diagnosed me as suffering from SAD: Sporting Anecdotes Disorder. Meanwhile my psychiatrist describes me as suffering from 'GAA Foot and Mouth'. On the other hand my therapist claims I suffer from ASS: Addicted to Sports Syndrome.

First a few words of warning. There are books of truth. There are books of fact. This is not one of them. This will not be a publication for anoraks because my aim was neither veracity nor accuracy. Quentin Crisp wrote: 'There are three reasons for becoming a writer: the first is that you need the money; the second that you have something to say that you think the whole world should know; the third is that you can't think what to do with the long winter evenings.' My sole agenda was to try and put a smile on people's faces. I dedicated my time and energy to finding the funniest GAA quotations and anecdotes and where there were debates about who said what I focused on what was said rather than spending exhaustive research on who said it. No story was too apocryphal for consideration if it was funny. My attitude was that if it was funny enough it just might be true enough!

Tribunal watchers reared on a diet of the truth, the whole truth and nothing but the truth will despair at this book because in this context it was humour that was sacrosanct. It is often said that truth is the first casualty of war. In some case truth may have been a casualty in these pages as the agenda to entertain took precedence.

Many of the stories in this collection are strange but true. However, the veracity of some of the stories would not measure up to that expected in a court of law. These stories are based on real events. Only the facts have been changed. I was trying to write a book that would be more hysterical than historical.

This book celebrates the great GAA comedians, although much of the time the humour is unintentional. Everybody who is anybody in gaelic games is here from Christy Ring to Ger Loughnane; from Joe Brolly to Joe Kernan; from Babs Keating to Pat Spillane; from John O'Mahony to John in the pub; from Angela Downey to that well-known GAA fan Kylie Minogue; and from Shane Curran to Buffy the Vampire Slayer.

CHAPTER ONE

Thy Kingdom Come

Of the many tributes paid to Páidí Ó Sé after the shocking news of his death emerged the most eloquent was penned by Colm O'Rourke: 'Another great oak has tumbled in the Kerry forest with Páidí Ó Sé taking the long sleep.' O'Rourke went on to add: 'An hour in Páidí Ó Sé's company at any time left a person feeling better about the world.' I know what he meant, however the Kerry legend was the most frustrating interviewee I ever met. I tried the front door, the back door, the side door but nothing would persuade him to reveal anything about his relationship with Maurice Fitzgerald.

Once I had bowed to the inevitable and conceded defeat the anecdotes flowed. My favourites were his accounts of the famous world tour after Kerry's historic four-in-a-row in 1981. Páidí began the celebrations before anyone else. He turned to Jack O'Shea immediately after Jacko sealed the trip with the decisive goal against Offaly in the 1981 All-Ireland and said: 'We're going to Australia.'

Although Páidí gave me the memorable image of himself and Seán Walsh filling a bath full of beer cans and eating salmon and quaffing champagne at the races my favourite was his account of the Bomber Liston's birthday celebration in Melbourne. Páidí relished the joy on the Bomber's face when he presented him with a television as a present. It was days later that the Bomber discovered Páidí had nicked the television from the hotel room next door.

MORE THAN WORDS

When he wanted to Páidí could shoot from the hip. A case in point was his verdict on playing against the Dubs: 'Psychopaths, in the best possible sense.'

Asked about Mick O'Connell, Páidí replied: 'He was a Maurice Fitzgerald. He would pull, if he had it, a white rabbit out of the hat.'

Páidí had his critics, some of the them were severe, but it never fazed him: 'It seems that if you wear your heart on your sleeve, well you're a thick f**ker.' Pat Spillane hit the nail on the head when he described his former teammate as 'a rogue in the best sense of the term'.

MISTAKEN IDENTITY

It was indeed right and fitting that Páidí's funeral Mass should have been punctuated with laughter, like when his brother remarked that all of Páidí's friends like CJ Haughey had the X Factor. He went on to recall that Páidí's favourite television programme was *Tonight with Vincent Browne*. Whenever Vincent asked a hapless politician a particularly difficult question Páidí would turn to the assembled crowd in his pub and say with his famed mischievous glint in his eye: 'This is how I'd get out of that one ...'

The biggest laugh though came when Páidí's nephew and All-Star footballer Tomás recalled his uncle's excitement each time the team bus would get close to Croke Park. He cited the example of a day when he was managing Westmeath. When they got into the dressing room Páidí sat down beside one of the lads and said: 'Jesus, you have to get out in front of your man quicker than the last day. The ball was going in fast and you were hanging back. You weren't coming out.'

His conversation partner looked at him stoically and said: 'Páidí, I'm the physio.'

VIPs

Another of Páidí's nephews, Darragh Ó Sé, tells the story of a fortnight before he died, four choppers landed in the field behind the pub. They were a gang home from London to play golf in Waterville and stopped off for some liquid refreshment. Páidí was thrilled at their arrival because of the fun he could knock out of the story of the choppers. For the next few days he was telling everyone in the locality that he had received an offer from a 'big county' to go back into management. When anyone asked him if it was serious Páidí's reply was: 'Serious? Sure didn't they send four choppers down to make it.'

MAMMYS' BOYS

Darragh also tells that one of Páidí's ploys as Kerry manager was to gather the names and numbers of the mothers of all the players. He would send them Christmas cards in the belief that if he got the mothers onside the sons would follow. Just for a laugh though the day after a Munster final win he would ring the mother of one of the players, in the certain knowledge he was on the lash, to see what kind of excuse the mother would come up with for her son.

HOLLYWOOD ROYALTY

Another of Darragh's stories was about the time a family friend brought Páidí and himself to the home of Hollywood icon Gregory Peck in Los Angeles. Páidí quickly got bored with Peck's anecdotes and in the middle of reciting his lines from *Moby Dick* cut him down in his prime when he asked: 'You have nothing like a bottle of Miller or something handy there, Gregory?'

To add fuel to the fire when Darragh asked him if he wanted his picture taken with Gregory's Oscar he replied: 'Not at all, I'm grand. Sure haven't I the All-Stars at home?'

THE FAMOUS FIVE

Páidí is part of an illustrious quintet, the 'magnificent five', with Ger Power, Mike Sheehy, Pat Spillane and Denis Moran, who won eight All-Ireland medals with Kerry, captaining the team to All-Ireland glory in 1985. In his fourteen years on the Kerry team he won five consecutive All-Stars from 1981 to 1985. However, his most impressive statistic is that in the ten All-Ireland finals he played in, he conceded just one point to his immediate opponent, David Hickey of Dublin in 1976.

His passion for football was evident at an early stage after Kerry beat Meath in the 1970 All-Ireland final. Páidí was a boarder so it was not possible for him to legitimately attend the homecoming celebrations. He arranged to borrow a bike from one of the day students, robbed a brush and dressed it up as a decoy in his bed and set out for Rathmore. When he returned the College dean, Dermot Clifford, now Archbishop of Cashel, was waiting for him at the entrance. 'Ó Sé, there are more brains in that brush above than in your head.'

CAREER CHANGE

In his later years on the Kerry team Mick O'Dwyer transformed Páidí from a pillaging right half-back into a tenacious corner-back. Con Houlihan compared the restriction of his attacking talents to 'tying a spaniel to a concrete block'.

THE WEST WING

Páidí enjoyed the company of famous people. Of the many photos on the 'wall of fame' in his pub in Ventry was one he had taken with Martin Sheen. Initially Páidí had not recognised 'the best president America never had'. When he was told the *West Wing* star was in the pub he asked: 'Who the f**k is Martin Sheen?' When he was given a summary of Sheen's career his response was typical of the man: 'F**k!' The great footballer rushed to effusively greet the great actor. As Sheen departed Páidí had an unusual request: 'Next time you see Tom Cruise, will you tell him I was asking for him?'

Shortly after a letter in Ventry arrived from Sheen which concluded: 'PS Tom says hello.'

Páidí was much more forthcoming when I asked him about Tom Cruise: 'He was a lovely, quiet fella and he was very interested in the finer points of gaelic football.'

Páidí also had possibly the most unusual duet in music history. He performed 'An Poc ar Buile' with Dolly Parton in the pub in Ventry.

FEAR CRUA

The great American sports writer, Red Smith said: 'I went to a fight and an ice hockey match broke out.' One of the most famous tours in rugby history was that of the Lions to South Africa in 1974. On the pitch the tour saw some very physical exchanges. One of the props on the tour, Gloucester's Mike Burton was well able to look after himself in these situations. The following year he became the first English international to be sent off in a Test match, following a clash with Australian winger Doug Osbourne. In the canon of sports literature Burton's autobiography *Never Stay Down* stands out. He devotes a chapter on the best punches he encountered in his career!

Páidí also had a reputation as a *fear crua*. This stemmed from his first Munster final when he was marking Cork's Dinny Allen. Dinny started the match well and kicked an early point. He triumphantly turned to his opponent and said: 'They'll be taking you off now shorty.' Páidí's reply has become a Youtube sensation. He hit Allen with a left hook.

On another occasion Kerry were playing the Dubs in a League match in Croke Park. Páidí was marking what he described to me as a 'prominent Dub' who turned to him in his finest city accent as they took their positions and said: 'Ye boys probably came up here on a tractor.' Páidí said nothing but he waited until the National Anthem and checked that the ref was looking elsewhere and then, he recalled to me, 'I bursshted him with a boxssh. He was on the ground calling for his mammy and I turned to him and said: "Jaysus Christ, you look like a lad that was knocked down by a tractor."'

Occupational Hazard

Páidí's own image of his playing style was probably best captured when he was casually asked on a trip to Sunderland what he did for a living. He replied quick as a flash: 'I make coffins for left half-forwards.'

Nose-y

When Dublin played Kerry in 1978 as a fundraiser for Sr Consilio's Cuan Mhuire rehabilitation centre the match was said to be the most physically violent in living memory. A lot of old scores had to be settled and markers were put down for the championship later that year. Pat O'Neill broke Jimmy Deenihan's nose. Afterwards O'Neill was very contrite and sent an apology later that night to Deenihan in the Kerry hotel. He told him he was very sorry and never intended to hurt him because he thought he was striking Páidí Ó Sé!

Do Not Disturb

Páidí was well able to tell stories against himself. Many go back to his time as a garda. In 1979 after a League match against Cork he went on the tear. The next morning when he went in to report for duty in Limerick he was feeling a bit off colour. He decided that the best way of concealing his discomfort was to take out the squad car and pretend to go on patrol but instead he pulled into a quiet field for a nap. A few hours later he was awoken by a great commotion and suddenly there were squad cars all over the field. Páidí stumbled out of the car to find himself face to face with the Assistant Commissioner who said, 'Páid, did you nod of for a little while?'

'I'm sorry. I'd an auld game yesterday and I just pulled in for a few minutes. What are all of ye doing here?'

'We're checking out the venue for the Pope's visit to Limerick next September. The Holy Father'll be saying a Mass out here. We're sussin' out the place for the security plan. Sorry to have disturbed you.'

Player Power

In 1985 everyone on the Kerry team had their heart set on winning the All-Ireland again. None more so than Páidí as he was captain. As Páidí was trying to gee up the troops before the game he said:

'We really need to win this one.'

Mick O'Dwyer asked: 'For who?'

'For me.'

'Not for Kerry?'

'Well, for Kerry as well.'

LAST ORDERS

Páidí always enjoyed the social side of the game. In the 1970s and 1980s winning All-Irelands became such a routine that as they ran on to Croke Park for the All-Ireland final, after Mick O'Dwyer had been trying to psyche the Kerry players up to play the game of their lives, John Egan ran up and pulled Páidí Ó Sé by the togs and asked him, 'Where are ye going after the game, Páid?'

SPORTING ECUMENISM

As Ireland went soccer mad during Italia '90 a mischievous journalist rang Páidí to ask him what he thought. With characteristic poise the legend dismissively replied: 'I've very little interest in soccer.'

SO THIS IS CHRISTMAS

Before his managerial success with Kerry seniors Páidí coached UCC. Over the Christmas period he brought the panel to Ventry for a three-day training camp, putting up the players in his own home and the houses of his family nearby. On the very first morning they were running on the beach by nine. As they ran down from Church Cross Páidí regaled them with local folklore. He told them that they were standing on the ancient site of Cath Fhionntra, where, according to legend, Fionn mac Cumhaill defeated the King of the World. As they moved along the beach, their manager showed the students a river where, he observed, Diarmuid and Grainne had shared moments of passionate intensity. As the students drank in the mysticism and the mythology they were quickly brought back down to earth when Páidí barked: 'Now lads, do ye see the next river beyond that? If ye don't get to that f**king river in less than eight minutes I'll eat the heads off ye.'

Sleeping Beauty

Páidí's style was to fight fire with fire. When he became Kerry manager one of the inner circle was wont to make a storm in a teacup about many small logistic issues. At first Páidí took no action. Then he discovered that the person concerned loved to go to bed early. Páidí took his revenge by regularly ringing him late at night, pretending to be deeply worried about some minor issue.

Speed Merchant

After Páidí attended an Ulster final in Clones he was less than pleased to find himself in a five-mile tailback. Lateral thinking was called for and Páidí's solution was to activate the hazard lights and drive as fast as possible in the opposite lane because motorists would imagine there was an emergency no one would stop him. Oncoming traffic politely diverted into ditches and driveways and in no time Páidí was safely in his destination.

Legacy

Páidí loved verbal jousting. He has already left a rich legacy to GAA folklore as the source and object of some quotes that will live long in the memory. These include:

Clare fan: Is the glass half-empty or half-full?
Páidí: It depends on whether you're drinking or pouring.

We're just off for a quiet pint. Then about twenty loud ones.

They think we're just a crowd of ignorant culchies from the bog. Let's not disappoint them.

Páidí psyches up Kerry before facing the Dubs.

David Hickey (before Dublin played Kerry in 1975): Welcome to Hell.
Páidí Ó Sé: True, but meet the Devil.

Dessie Dolan before a flight: Look here Páidí if it's your day to go, it's your day to go.
Páidí: But if it's the f**king pilot's day to go, he's going to bring me down with him!

Páidí to Westmeath player: For f**k's sake, will you go up for the ball.
Player: Sure won't it come down to me.

IN THE HOT SEAT
Páidí's finest hour as a manager came when he led Kerry to the 1997 All-Ireland. That was the game when Maurice Fitzgerald regularly broke through the Mayo defenders, as they fell around him like dying wasps, and kicked incredible points from all angles. Páidí led Kerry to another All-Ireland in 2000 following a replay against Galway.

The wheels came off the wagon though in the 2001 All-Ireland semi-final when Meath beat Kerry by no less than fifteen points. Kerry went through a twenty-nine minute spell in the first half without scoring and then could only muster a single point from substitute Declan Quill in the second half. After the match Marty Morrissey asked a Kerry fan: 'Where did it all go wrong in Croke Park today?'

The fan replied: 'The green bit in the middle.'

MAGIC MOMENTS
A letter to *The Kerryman* newspaper praised Páidí's special powers: 'In Kerry we have not had much to be proud of lately but we like to think Páidí is the greatest magician of all time. He made

24

Kerry disappear for the entire second half of the 2002 All-Ireland final against Armagh.'

An old joke revised:
   'Why aren't the Kerry team allowed to own a dog?'
   'Because they can't hold on to a lead.'

The 2002 All-Ireland final was a classic case of *nouveau riche* versus old money that Kerry fans will never be allowed to forget – don't think they haven't tried. At half-time Kerry seemed to be cruising against Armagh but the Kerry lads snatched defeat from the jaws of victory. A few weeks later a man was driving home from a night in the pub. He was pulled in by a guard. The officer said: 'I'm going to have to get you to blow into the bag.'

   The driver pulled out a card from his pocket which read: 'Asthmatic. Don't take breath samples.'

   The garda said: 'I'm going to have to take a sample of your blood.'

   He took out a card from his pocket: 'Hemophiliac. Don't take blood samples.'

   The garda said: 'I'm going to have to take a urine sample.'

   The motorist took out another card from his pocket. This one read: 'Member of Kerry supporters club. Don't take the piss.'

CRIMINAL MATTERS

When it seemed that things could get no worse Kerry people sat at home in 2003 and watched Tyrone destroy the Kingdom in the All-Ireland semi-final. Two Tralee men had a revealing conversation: 'I saw the Kerry team on television last night with the Sam Maguire trophy.'

   'What programme was it?'

   '*Crimeline.*'

MORE THAN WORDS

2003 was Páidí's year of the U-turn. In January he gave an interview with the *Sunday Independent* and famously said: 'Being the Kerry manager is probably the hardest job in the world because Kerry people, I'd say, are the roughest type of f**king animals you could deal with. And you can print that.'

A short time later he was forced to meekly apologise: 'I regret very much if I have offended all or some of my Kerry supporters who have been very loyal to me.'

MAROONED

When he became manager of Westmeath in 2004 apart from his strong language some of the players found Páidí's stories a little baffling. One was about the seaman who met a pirate and noticed that he had a peg leg, a hook, and an eye patch. 'So how did you end up with a peg leg?' the seaman asked. 'I was swept overboard and a shark bit my leg off,' the pirate replied. 'What about your hook?' asked the seaman. 'Well, we were boarding an enemy ship and one of the enemy cut my hand off,' the pirate said. 'So how did you get the eye patch?' the seaman finally asked. 'I got something in my eye,' replied the pirate. When the sailor looked confused, the pirate continued: 'It was my first day with the hook.'

To this day the Westmeath players are still trying to figure out what point he was trying to make with the story.

SOUR GRAPES

Páidí had his critics and sometimes they didn't pull their punches:

Páidí Ó Sé took the defeat very badly – so badly in fact that on the Tuesday of the defeat he rang the Samaritans. When they heard who it was they hung up.

Clare fan.

He's not so much a coach as a hearse.

A frustrated Maurice Fitzgerald fan on Páidí.

In future Cork should play all their home games against Kerry in Fota Wild Life Park to make the Kerry fans feel at home.

Cork fan after the 'f**king animals' controversy.

GET SMART

Páidí was known for his keen intelligence. This trait was evident from an early age if a story heard in Templenoe is to be believed. When he was a young man he entered the confessional box and said, 'Bless me, Father, for I have sinned. I have been with a loose woman.'

The priest asks, 'Is that you Páidí?'

'Yes, Father, it is.'

'And who was the woman you were with?'

'Sure and I can't be telling you, Father. I don't want to ruin her reputation.'

'Well, Páidí, I'm sure to find out sooner or later, so you may as well tell me now. Was it Mary?'

'I cannot say.'

'Was it Monica?'

'I'll never tell.'

'Was it Lizzie?'

'I'm sorry, but I'll not name her.'

'Was it Patsy?'

'My lips are sealed.'

'Was it Fiona, then?'

'Please, Father, I cannot tell you.'

The priest sighs in frustration, 'You're a steadfast lad, Páidí, and I admire that. But you've sinned, and you must atone. Be off with you now.'

Páidí walked back to his pew. Pat Spillane slid over and whispered, 'What you get?'

'Five good leads,' said Páidí.

COMMON SENSE

The Secret Footballer has become compulsive reading because of his series of perceptive insights into the world of English football, and in 2012 his book was voted sports book of the year. He describes going to see his young son play his first schoolboy match. Just before kick-off he had an urge to shout something inspirational to his flesh and blood. He roared, 'JUST DON'T BE SH*T, OK?'

TLC

One of Páidí O'Sé's stories was about a Kerry footballer of yesteryear who was in serious need of some love and affection but he had no wife nor money. So one evening he met a lady of the night in Tralee and asked her the cost of her services. When he explained he had no money she inquired if he had anything in his pockets. He replied that he had two All-Ireland medals. As it was a slow night she agreed to exchange her services for the two medals.

A few weeks later some Mayo footballers came to Tralee on a stag night. One of their number met the same lady of the night. The conversation unfolded as follows:

'How much do your charge?'

'200 euro.'

'That's an awful lot.'

'But I'm worth it.'

'How do I know you are any good?'

'Here. Let me show you my two All-Ireland medals.'

CHAPTER TWO

Spat Spillane

If someone said to me ten years ago that I would become friends with Pat Spillane I would have laughed at them because where I come from in Roscommon they speak of Pat in the same way they speak of toxic waste.

It's not because he's spent the last twenty-five years slagging off Connacht football – though he has – it all goes back to his 'performance' in the 1980 All-Ireland. After eleven minutes of the game Roscommon had the great Kerry team on the run and were leading 1–2 to no score and really rolling. Eventually the ball found its way into the Kerry forward line. As Pat made his way towards the goal, one of the Roscommon backs 'lightly brushed' against him and Pat went down like a bag of spuds. Now I don't want to say he was down a long time: but the next morning I was talking to my neighbour, Paddy Joe. The poor man's cow was calving shortly before the match and he could not leave for the game until his brand new Charolais bull calf was born. So as soon as the calf was out Paddy Joe jumped into his glamorous car – a Morris Minor – and turned on the car radio. He was in Tyrellspass when the match started and was just passing Harry's in Kinnegad when Pat went down injured. As he drove on he heard how Pat was rolling to the right and rolling to the left. Just as Paddy Joe took his place in the Hogan Stand Pat finally got up.

Within seconds Pat was flying up and down the wing like a March hare and setting up the goal for Mike Sheehy that turned the match. Ever since then we say in Roscommon that the two worst things about Pat Spillane are – his face.

In Tyrone they call him 'Puke' but in Roscommon we call him 'Pepper' because he always gets up your nose. In return for sharing his insights about football in recent years I gave hime the benefit of my knowledge on other subjects: I tried to educate him about a healthy diet. He thought sugar diabetes was a Welsh heavyweight boxer.

A MOTHER'S LOVE

I felt though it was my duty for this book to provide readers with an objective assessment of Pat. The only problem was where I would get it from. I couldn't ask anyone from Mayo. They all hate him there. I couldn't ask anyone from Kildare. They all really hate him there. And I certainly couldn't ask anyone from Ulster – they despise him there. In the end Pat indirectly gave me the answer himself about the best objective assessment because, as we all know, one of Pat's most famous comments as an analyst were about his mother's arthritis and the Armagh full-back line. So I decided to ask my mother what she thought of Pat. She said: 'Oh, Pat Spillane, eight All-Ireland medals, nine All-Stars, twice player of the year, he had everything you could possibly want in a footballer; except two things – talent and good looks.'

HOLDING OUT FOR A HERO

But seriously getting to know Pat has been a very educational experience for me. People often say you should never meet your heroes; what I have learned though is that you should always meet your anti-hero because in the last ten years I have discovered there is a lot more to Pat than the crotchety character we see on television. Although we have different personalities, and even more radically different views on Connacht football, we share a lot of biases, prejudices and tastes. One of our shared idiosyncrasies is a fondness for compiling lists. So I thought I would include the top ten Pat Spillane qualities. The problem is I could not think of ten, so I had to limit it to two! In inverse order they are:

2. He is very decisive. I would go as far as to say he's the most decisive and emphatic person I've ever met. He never, ever has any doubts – he's usually wrong – but he never has any doubts.

1. He is well able to laugh at himself – some people would say that's probably a good thing, as there's so much to laugh at.

GRUMPY OLD MAN

The former Scottish centre-half Gordon McQueen once said unfairly of Frank Stapleton that he gets up in the morning and smiles at himself in the mirror just to get it out of the way for the day. Those of us who know him understand that this is not the case for Pat Spillane but many fans think of him as a grumpy old man because of his performances on *The Sunday Game*.

Given his penchant for controversy, an RTÉ announcer made an interesting slip of the tongue when she introduced Pat as 'Spat Spillane' in 2009. True to form Spillane took it in his stride and said: 'I've been called worse.'

Much, much worse.

AN EDDIE HOBBS MOMENT

Pat's passion for the game is still as strong today as in his playing days. I saw this at first hand watching him filling in a credit card application form. When it came to the question that asked 'What is your position in the company?' he answered 'Left half-forward'.

TRIUMPH AND TRAGEDY

In any discussion on the greatest players of all time Spillane's name is sure to figure prominently. He won eight All-Ireland medals and was one of the biggest stars of the legendary Kerry team of the 1970s and 1980s. In rural Ireland parlance he didn't pick up his talent 'off the trees'. The footballing genes were prominent in his DNA. His late father, Tom, was himself a Kerry footballer as were his uncles the Lynes, Jackie and Dinny, who won All-Ireland medals for Kerry.

To add to Pat's treasure trove of golden memories he was joined on the great Kerry team by his brothers, Mick and Tom. The Spillanes were not just part of Irish sporting history they were also centre stage in one of Ireland's greatest religious occasions.

Early in 1979, news broke that the Pope would visit Ireland that September. As thousands of pilgrims waited on Galway racecourse on a misty September Sunday morning they laughed heartily at Bishop Eamonn Casey's warm-up performance, a roller coaster of fun and frolics. During the Papal Mass for the youth of Ireland Spillane's brother Mick made a presentation as part of the giving of gifts.

Pat has always had the gift of the gab. In August 2003 Kerry walking champion Gillian O'Sullivan's single-minded determination reaped a handsome dividend when she won a silver medal in the World Championships in Paris. However, she did not perhaps get the credit she deserved because walking is not a glamorous sport. Most of the sporting headlines that day were created by Tyrone's demolition of Kerry in the All-Ireland football semi-final. Spillane commented typically on a mixed day for the Kingdom. 'We saw a great day for Kerry sport when Gillian O'Sullivan won a silver medal in the European Championships.

Then that same afternoon we saw Kerry implode against Tyrone in the All-Ireland semi-final. It was like winning the Lotto and then immediately finding out that you had only twenty-four hours to live!'

Sunny Side Up

Spillane was invited by RTÉ to compete in their inaugural Sports Superstars championship to be recorded early in 1979. He joined Limerick hurler Pat Hartigan, Arsenal footballer Dave O'Leary, swimmer David Cummins, Formula One driver Derek Daly, athlete Noel Carroll, Dublin footballer Jimmy Keaveney, boxer Mick Dowling and Cork's Jimmy Barry-Murphy. To give a light touch to the proceedings, the sports personalities were divided into teams each made up of two 'superathletes', one female athlete, one personality and one politician. Personalities who agreed to take part included Fr Michael Cleary, Frank Kelly and Dickie Rock. After Spillane won the competition he took part in the World Superstars competition in the Bahamas. He did not know much about protecting himself from the sun and as a result of his pink visage and body a new phrase entered popular currency, 'Spillane tan'!

Miracle Recovery

'Is Pat Spillane really hurt or is he in line for an Oscar?' So Micheál O'Hehir wondered aloud during the 1980 All-Ireland final. Roscommon's Gerry Fitzmaurice and Spillane were involved in an incident off the ball. Pat was prostrate on the ground and took an age to get up. Time went by and many efforts were made to assist his recovery, to no avail. About four minutes later Pat staggered up. It did not escape the fans' attention that Roscommon were playing with a strong wind at the time.

Spillane knows he has never been forgiven by the Rossies:

My scathing comments about the Roscommon forward line down the years were not to go unpunished throughout the county. A story went around Roscommon about a visit I had to my home from Mick O'Dwyer. As I was getting so much hate mail at the time from disgruntled Roscommon fans I had acquired two new dogs for protection. Micko asked me what their names were. I responded by saying that one was named 'Rolex' and the other was named 'Timex'.

Dwyer asked, 'Whoever heard of someone naming dogs like that?'

'Hello,' I answered. 'They're watch dogs!'

DOCTOR KNOWS BEST

Spillane was one of the many players who made trips to America to play in the New York championship. It was an ideal opportunity to make a few dollars and have a holiday. Big name stars over from Ireland were always subject to 'robust' play on the field. On one occasion this necessitated Spillane visiting the medical room with blood pouring from his nose. An Italian doctor was on duty and was more interested in reading the *New York Times* than attending to Spillane. Without looking up from his paper he asked the footballer what was wrong. The Kerry star said, 'I think I've broken my nose.' With no concern in his voice the doctor told him to go over to the mirror and clean off the blood. When this task was completed the doctor inquired, 'Does it look different than it did this morning?' Spillane replied, 'Yes, it's crooked.' The doctor calmly replied, 'You probably broke your nose then.' Thus ended the medical consultation.

We're all going on a Summer Holiday

Exotic tours abroad were a feature of Spillane's life with the great Kerry teams of the 1970s and 1980s. In 1986 Mick O'Dwyer brought them on a holiday to the Canaries. It was mainly for rest and recreation but there was a small element of training. Every evening at 5 p.m. the players met for a run along the sand dunes of Playa de Inglés. Part of the beach was reserved as a nudist section. Spillane remarked that when the Kerry players reached that section of the beach the pace dropped alarmingly!

Four years earlier O'Dwyer brought the Kerry team for a run on a beach in San Fransisco the day after they had given a horrendous performance against the All-Stars. The display was the legacy of a day-long drinking session by some of the squad at Fisherman's Wharf on the eve of the match. The most revealing evidence of the commitment of the Kerry players to the cause was that the first man home on the beach run was the president of the GAA, Seán Kelly, then chairman of the Kerry County Board.

Are You Being Served?

In 1981 after completing the historic four-in-a-row of All-Ireland titles the Kerry team went on the holiday of a lifetime to America, Hawaii and Australia. They were booked into a hotel in Adelaide in Australia after a long overnight flight. Shortly after, an irate member of the Kerry delegation rang down to complain about the lack of air conditioning in his room. He threatened to pull the entire Kerry party out of the hotel if the problem was not fixed immediately. A member of staff arrived up to the room and took a quick glance before looking the man with a complaint in the eye and coolly said, 'Why not try and plug it in buddy?'

TIPSTER

On that tour Spillane was reputed to have taken a taxi back to the team's hotel with a few of the other players after a drinking session one evening. The taxi driver was a bit obese and was also 'hygienically-challenged', with a less than enticing aroma emanating from his body. In addition he recounted a tale of woe about his lack of success with the opposite sex. After the Kerry lads paid their fare the taxi driver said, 'How about a tip?'

Before anyone could even think of reaching to their pockets for a second time Spillane is said to have interjected, 'Certainly. Start using a deodorant and you might have some chance with the women.'

CLOSER TO HOME

In 1982 Kerry planned a trip to Bali to celebrate what had been expected to be their five-in-a-row. After sensationally losing the final to Offaly the Kerry players were saying that the only Bali they would be going to was Ballybunion! They also said, 'It won't even be the Canaries this year. All we'll get is the Seagulls.'

WHEN PAT NEARLY MET CHARLIE

Collegiality was a feature of that Kerry team as Spillane acknowledges:

> I was great friends with Páidí Ó Sé. I marvelled at the way he could make friends with people like Charlie Haughey. They had a lot in common. Neither were short on self-confidence. Charlie presented himself as a great statesman on the world stage. Mind you Páidí himself did not believe that you should hide your light under a bushel. A visitor to his pub observed that only a North Korean dictator had as many photos of themselves as Páidí did. The local taximan when he took tourists from America to Páidí's always told them that the

church beside the pub was built as a shrine to Páidí. When they saw all the photos in the pub they believed him.

Páidí captained Kerry to the All-Ireland in 1984. The following morning Páidí brought my brother, Tom, and a few of the other lads out to meet Charlie in Kinsealy. Sadly though I missed out on my own meeting with Charlie Haughey. I came very close. I was in the Schelig Hotel the morning after the Dingle Regatta and Charlie and his entourage were quaffing champagne. They were loud and boisterous and I heard one of them say: 'There's Pat Spillane over there.'

Charlie swanned over to the table beside me and tapped the man on the shoulder and said: 'Pat Spillane I presume.'

The astonished guy replied: 'I wish.'

Charlie turned on his heels and walked back to his party as if nothing happened. So much for his great knowledge of Kerry football.

SHOOTING FROM THE LIP

After his retirement as a footballer Spillane turned his talents to working in the media. Not everyone welcomes having a microphone stuck under their face. The legendary Kerry footballer Ger Power was once asked a question in the build-up to a big match. He replied, 'Whatever I said last year, put me down for the same again this time.'

Spillane was much more comfortable in that environment. Apart from his genius on the field Spillane changed the face of punditry in the GAA with his straight-talking style. A small illustration came after his beloved Kerry team lost to Cork in the Munster semi-final replay in 2009: 'You know that great piece of Irish literature we were all subjected to when we went to school, *Peig*. Her opening line about herself was that she was an old woman now, with one leg on the bank and the other in the grave – and in a way it could sum up this Kerry football team.'

He immediately carved out a reputation for telling it as it is and pulling no punches. At the mention of some journalists he gives a look which suggests he supports George Bernard Shaw's advice not to 'waste time on people who don't know what they think'.

His desire to be brutally honest has not always been appreciated. At various times he has annoyed, among others, all football fans in Kildare, Mayo and practically every county in Ulster. His derisory comments about the Kildare team in 2001 prompted Ted Walsh to say to him, 'The real problem with the foot and mouth epidemic Pat is that you didn't get it.' A lot of experts were talking up Tyrone's chances for the All-Ireland in 2002. This trend accelerated after they won the National League that year. Spillane immediately cast cold water on that proposition by pointing out that it was a meaningless barometer of their prospects for the championship, 'You get more contact in an old time waltz at an old folks home than in a National League final.' He also dismissed Cavan's chances, 'They have a forward line that couldn't punch holes in a paper bag.'

A STRANGER ON A TRAIN

One of the most memorable train journeys this writer ever experienced was shortly after the '97 All-Ireland. I found myself sitting beside a man of mature years, who was puffing away on his pipe. Given his disposition I thought at first he might be a parish priest. The conversation quickly turned to football and he gave an incisive critique of the problems of Connacht football. Then he turned to the media reportage of teams from the West. Immediately he had a transformation of Dr Jekyll and Mr Hyde proportions. He reeled off a litany of names of journalists and pundits and what he proposed to do with them can not be reprinted on the grounds of public order and morality. After his vicious tirade he paused for a deep breath. A pregnant pause ensued before he said more in sorrow than in anger, 'F**k them all bar Spillane.'

I nearly fell of my seat. I heard myself ask incredulously, 'Why do you say bar Spillane?'

'Ah sure, young fella, Spillane is f**ked already.'

Wrong Place

Spillane, though, was not the renowned Kerry footballer of yesteryear who famously was the guest speaker at a dinner of a major club in Mayo. The star launched into a passionate speech as to why the club he named was one of the top clubs in the country. After a few minutes into his speech he knew that the audience reaction was much less warm than he anticipated. He discovered that he was talking about the wrong club! He excused himself and said he had to go the toilet. He never returned.

Future Imperfect

Despite his unique insight into gaelic games, which comes from being one of the greatest footballers of all time and winning eight All-Irelands, Pat does not always get his predictions right. At half-time in the 2002 All-Ireland final he was 'sceptical' about Armagh's chances of beating Kerry. He caused consternation among Armagh fans when he said, 'My mother has arthritis but even she has more pace than the Armagh full-back line.' In the second half Pat was left eating humble pie. Understandably, one banner, featured prominently in the subsequent media coverage, said, against a backdrop of the Armagh colours, 'Are you watching Pat Spillane?'

Three days later when Armagh played Louth in the GOAL challenge a large man dressed up in drag, in the Kerry colours, and wearing a placard reading: 'Pat Spillane's Ma' challenged each of the full-back line to an individual race. 'She' won each time. The players weren't trying.

THE BEGINNING OF WISDOM

Getting predictions wrong does not phase Spillane unduly. On such occasions he always quotes the lines of the Declan Nerney song:

> If I knew then what I knew now
> I'd be a wiser man.

He is philosophical about his errors, 'The great thing is that RTÉ pay me to come and tell the nation what I think will happen. Then when I make a dog's dinner of it and get it badly wrong the *Sunday World* pay me the following Sunday to explain why I got it so wrong!'

JEEPERS KEEPERS

In July 2002 the *Sunday World* asked Spillane to do player profiles of everyone due to play in the All-Ireland quarter-finals. With eight teams involved they wanted him to write pen-pictures of a hundred and twenty players. That is a pretty difficult exercise. When you have to write about sixteen corner-backs it is very hard to find sixteen different ways of saying 'tight-marker' and 'tenacious'.

His problems began though with the goalkeepers. There are not too many things you can say about a goalie other than he is a 'good shot-stopper', 'has great reflexes', and 'has a good kick-out'. Generally the only variable is whether you can use 'very agile'. By the time he got to the last goalkeeper on the list, Armagh's Benny Tierney, Spillane was getting very bored with repeating himself so he described him as 'fat and overweight'. Benny came up with a great retort. He said. 'Spillane is right. Yes I am fat and overweight now but he will always be ugly.'

Spillane took the insult in good spirit: 'I salute Benny for keeping a bit of humour in the game and I just wish there were a few more like him up north.'

SICK BAY

Spillane's most famous feat of punditry came in 2003 when he described Tyrone's performance in their All-Ireland triumph over Kerry as 'puke football'. His remark provoked a tidal wave of indignation. Happily there were a few gems among all the vitriol: 'Spillane's comment about puke football should be interpreted as Pure Unadulterated Kerry Embarrassment.'

The *pièce de résistance* though has got to be: 'Pat Spillane, what can you expect from a sickening dose but "puke"?' Little wonder then that there's a joke still doing the rounds in Tyrone:

Q. Why does Pat Spillane open yoghurt pots while still in the supermarket?
A. Because the lid says 'Open Here'.

DONEGAL CATCH

In 2011 Spillane was in the firing line with his repeated criticism of Donegal's negative tactics. One habit that football fans have in Donegal since is slagging Spillane off. Typical of this was a Ballybofey fan's summation of his football career: 'Pat Spillane had the speed of a racehorse, the strength of a plough-horse and the brains of a rocking horse.'

ON THE BLANKET ON THE GROUND

Spillane blames what he sees as the negativity in Ulster football on video analysis and blanket defences: 'I am sick of watching games in Croke Park where the only performers trying to play positively are the Artane Boys band.'

OUR FRIENDS IN THE NORTH

Amazingly Spillane is a popular choice for GAA clubs in Ulster as a guest speaker. Initially it was a cultural clash for him:

> I got a great insight into the Northern mentality at my first function in the North. It was a question and answer session in Coalisland in the early 1990s. You have to try and realise that they are coming at things from a totally different angle. I realised that when a fella put up his hand and asked me: 'Do you know why Jack O'Shea never catches the ball at the throw-in?'
>
> I was puzzled and said I did not. He continued: 'I'll tell you why. It is because Jacko has a contract with Adidas, a foreign company, and that's why he never catches the ball in case he'd be photographed with it.'
>
> In the circumstances, after I got over my initial shock at the suggestion, I thought the politic thing to say was, 'You could be right.'

KNOW YOUR PLACE

It would not be the last time Spillane was taken by surprise:

> I do a lot of after-dinner speeches. One of my worst experiences as an after-dinner speaker was up in Dungiven Hurling Club. If I was being well paid for it I wouldn't have minded but I was doing it as a favour for Joe Brolly. I arrived late. Everyone was plastered. The three hundred plus attendance was exclusively male. They were all in their monkey suits but there were lots of earrings and lots of tattoos. It was a very intimidating audience. I sat alongside the chief officer of the club who deeply resented that a football guy was here giving a speech. The former Offaly hurler Pat Delaney spoke before me. His speech was about patriotism, nationalism and how hurling was a thirty-two county sport and he extolled the joys of hurling. He

got an incredible response. I thought to myself that I had all my gags ready and believed this was going to be a real belter. As they were lapping up Delaney's speech I should have realised the writing was on the wall. I started into my speech and two minutes later a guy stood up and said: 'We don't like what you say about Ulster football.' He was quickly told to shut up. I thought to myself with my gags ready I was going to bring the crowd under control.

Five minutes later a different man got up and said: 'F**k you. We don't like what you say about Ulster football.' Thankfully one of my teammates from the International Rules football team, Brian Gilligan, got up and went down to him and told him to sit down. When big Brian tells you to sit down you sit down.

I plodded on and spoke for twenty-five minutes. I died a death. At the end of the speech the chairman got up and said: 'I'd just like to reiterate that the name of this club is not Dungiven Hurling Club. It's the Kevin Lynch Hurling Club.' With that he nearly lifted the roof because of the round of applause he got. Who was Kevin Lynch? I did not know then but I know now. He was one of the hunger strikers in 1981. To this day I hold onto the black biro that was presented to me that night with Kevin Lynch, Dungiven, written on it. A reminder of one of my bad days.

JUDICIAL MISCONDUCT

Spillane might have hoped things could not get any worse when he spoke in the future. Not for the first time, he was wrong:

My worst gig was in UCC Rugby Club. I was all excited when I got there. I was making my debut on the after-dinner circuit in the real capital – surely a passport to big bucks. I was doing it for a friend, a doctor in Cork. We went to a pre-dinner reception which was kindly sponsored by a drinks company. I drank lots of pints. My wife came with me and she was all set for a great night. I started my speech. It was going well. The students though got restless very quickly. I kept talking. Must finish my speech. The students were getting even more restless. More gags to go. I must finish my speech. I was dying a death. I was determined to finish when I noticed that even the people on the table alongside me were talking. In a drunken haze I turned to the man beside me and said: 'Excuse me, sir. If you want to talk, you come up here and talk.' It didn't go down well. How was I to know he was the local District Court Judge? Bad speech. My wife didn't talk to me for two days. She has never come to one of my after-dinner speeches since!

DOUBLE STANDARDS

Spillane was the main speaker at a major gala of a prominent club in Ulster. At the end of the night a spectator went up to the emcee for the evening, Adrian Logan from UTV, and said, ''Twas shocking to hear all that filthy language here this evening. That kind of talk has no place in the GAA.'

Adrian nodded and just to make conversation asked the man what he thought of Pat Spillane. Logan was surprised with his response, 'I can't stand that f**king c**t. He only talks sh*t*.'

THE LAST SUPPER

There were happier visits though to Ulster. In 1994 Pat did a function in Tyrone and in 2004 he returned to the same venue. His opening words of ten years previously were quoted back to him in full. Peter Canavan was in the audience in 1994 and Spillane began by saying: 'I look down the hall and I see before me Peter Canavan, one of the greatest Tyrone players of all time. They call

Peter Canavan "God" up here. They call me a boll*x. I have eight All-Ireland medals and Peter Canavan has none.'

THE MEMORY MAN

Spillane often reflects on his relationship with Ulster fans:

My problem with Ulster football is personal. They all hate me up there!' Jimmy Magee often relates the story from the days he was commentating on UTV when he was walking across the pitch in Clones after an Ulster football championship match when an Ulster football fan came up to him and said: 'Tell that boll*x Spillane he knows nothing about football.' Jimmy replied: 'Hang on a minute. He has eight All-Ireland medals and nine All-Star awards. He must know something about football.'

The man walked away muttering all kinds of obscenities and cast severe doubts on the Kerry star's parentage.

THE LAST LAUGH

Invariably, the Ulster fans have their own revenge on Spillane. They call him 'the funeral director' because they claim that he is always miserable looking. They also say: 'Remember the good old days when the only thing that annoyed you about television was poor reception. Now the reception is perfect but they sent us Pat Spillane to punish us instead.'

THANK YOU FOR THE MUSIC

Spillane has a particular place in the affections of Cork fans: 'In Cork at the very mention of my name they all burst into song. Mind you the song they sing is "The Langer"!'

Sharon Ní Bheoláin and the way she might look at you
Spillane sees the funny side of his TV profile:

> There is an amusing website which has a diary of a Kerry
> football pundit. According to this the only reason why I spend
> any time in RTÉ is to try and catch the eye of Sharon Ní
> Bheoláin. That's so untrue. Those of us fortunate enough to
> work in RTÉ Sport have no need to be drooling over Sharon.
> We have our very own sex symbol – Marty Morrissey!

Domestic Bliss

Every rose has its thorns. Being away from home every weekend
is not conducive to domestic bless. All marriages are happy. It's
the living together afterwards that causes all the trouble as
Spillane has found out to his cost:

> My wife accused me of loving gaelic football more than her.
> 'Yeah, but I love you more than hurling or rugby,' I replied.
> In fairness she did pay me a great compliment yesterday. She
> told me that I brought 'a little ray of sunshine' into her life. I
> was chuffed and asked her how. She took the wind out of my
> sails when she answered, 'When you came home last night
> from working on *The Sunday Game*, foaming at the mouth and
> muttering something about Ulster football, you slammed the
> door so hard that the Venetian blind fell off the window.'

Stud Down

I am reliably informed though that the most popular joke going
around the GAA websites involves Spillane walking into a sperm
donor bank and saying to the receptionist, 'I'd like to donate some
sperm.'

She asked him. 'Have you ever donated before?'

He replied. 'Yes. You should have my details on your computer.'

The receptionist said: 'Oh yes. But I see you're going to need help. Shall I get a lap dancer for you?'

'Why do I need help?' the Kerry legend asked.

The receptionist replied: 'Well, it said on your record that you're a useless w*nk*r.'

CHAPTER THREE

The Kingdom, the Power and the Glory

A man had a ticket for the All-Ireland final but was seated right at the top of the stand, in the corner, with the worst possible view of the pitch. As the match started he noticed one empty seat, beautifully positioned, exactly in front of the half-way line. Taking a chance, he raced down from the top of the stand, to where the spare seat was.

'Excuse me, Sir,' he said to the man sitting next to the empty seat. 'Is anybody sitting there?'

'No,' replied the man in an obvious Kerry accent. 'That seat is empty.'

'That's incredible, who in their right mind would have a seat like this for the All-Ireland final, and not use it?'

'Well, actually the seat belongs to me,' replied the Kerry man. 'I was supposed to be here with my wife but she passed away.'

'Oh, I'm sorry to hear that. That's terrible, but couldn't you find someone else – a friend or even a neighbour to take the seat?' The Kerry man shook his head.

'They've all gone to her funeral.'

This little story is a small indicator of just how seriously they take football in Kerry. Maybe that is why it is said that there are two kinds of people: those who are from Kerry and those who want to be from Kerry.

BLESS ME FATHER

Kerry football has produced many great characters, like Jackie Lyne. Jackie was a great player and produced three fine sons, who all played for the local club team. Two of their names were Jackie and Dinny; the third, who Jackie referred to as 'His Reverence', was ordained to the priesthood. Jackie always, always wore his hat. The only time the hat came off his head was during the consecration at Mass. After a club match Jackie was holding court in the pub reliving the crucial moment in the match. 'Dinny kicked the ball out. Jackie caught it and kicked it in to His Reverence.' He paused his dramatic narrative to lift his hat at the mention of 'His Reverence'. The religious aura though was quickly dissipated as he came to the climax: '… and he kicked it into the f**king goal.'

THE BAWN

It was Mae West who famously observed, 'A hard man is good to find.' In Kerry football they found one in Paddy 'Bawn' Brosnan. He was one of the all-time great Kerry footballers. His commitment to football was evident at an early age. Attending the local Christian Brothers school he was asked to conjugate the Latin verb *venio*. Paddy Bawn simply shrugged his shoulders and said, 'Ah sure Brother, I'm only here for the football.'

He played senior football for Kerry, winning thirteen Munster medals, three Railway Cups and All-Irelands in 1940, 1941 and 1946. He captained the team in the 1944 All-Ireland, only to lose to Jimmy Murray's Roscommon. One player who has never forgotten his encounter with 'the Bawn' that day is Roscommon's Brendan Lynch: 'I was marking the famous Paddy "Bawn" Brosnan. He was a fisherman and fond of the women, fond of the porter and fond of the rough and tumble!'

THE PRINCE OF POETS

One of John B.'s great friends was Brendan Kennelly, former Professor of English at Trinity College and arguably Ireland's best loved poet:

> John B. had some reservations about my career in academic life. He pointed out that at the time teachers were very respected but had very little money. John B. used to say that I would be better if I had a job with a little less respect and a little more money!
>
> As a child John B. was enthralled by lifting the Sam Maguire Cup and captaining the Kerry team to win the All-Ireland. So much was he exercised by this that when his mother brought him to Mass one Sunday as the priest lifted the chalice during the consecration John B. turned to her and whispered, 'Why does he get to win the cup every Sunday?'
>
> As a young man John B. was very serious about football to the extent that he decided to give up the drink for Lent as a sign of his commitment to the game. One Ash Wednesday John B. met his neighbour Micky Joe. In local parlance John B. was 'fond of a sup'. So Micky Joe was shocked when John B. told him that he was giving up drink for Lent. He then qualified his answer by saying 'except in emergencies'.
>
> 'What does that mean exactly?' asked Micky Joe.
>
> With a twinkle in his eye Master Keane replied, 'Well, someone might say, "What are you having John B.?"'

NO OBJECTION

John B. was a good footballer and a great admirer of the pride people took in playing club football in Kerry and he told a story to illustrate the point. Within hours of the tragic death of the corner-forward in a traffic accident, an ambitious young hopeful rang the local club chairman. 'I hope you don't mind me ringing at this time,' he said, 'but I was wondering whether I might take the place of the deceased ...'

'I hadn't really thought about it,' replied the chairman, 'but if the undertaker doesn't mind, then neither will I.'

FIERCESOME

John B. also told a story about a Kerry County junior football final. By the time the final was played most of the better players had returned to college as it was delayed due to the usual quota of objections. John B. claimed he was drafted in to play at corner-forward, even though he was only about fifteen years of age. He gave a vivid description of his increasing trepidation as he went to take up his position and saw a 'seasoned' corner-back advancing to meet him. John B. was getting more intimidated with each step but was puzzled when the corner-back veered off at the last moment and went back towards his goalkeeper. He took out his false teeth and loudly told his keeper: 'Paddy mind these in case I forget myself and eat someone.'

QUOTE, UNQUOTE

While Kerry footballers have given great entertainment down the years with their performances on the field sometimes their comments off it can be every bit as entertaining, as the following compilation indicates:

He was a man mountain – he would catch aeroplanes if it helped Kerry.

John B. Keane on Mick O'Connell.

What they say about Cork footballers being ignorant is rubbish. I spoke to a couple yesterday and they were quite intelligent.

Brendan Kennelly.

A Kerry footballer with an inferiority complex is one who thinks he's just as good as everybody else.

John B. Keane.

How would you know a Cork footballer? He's the one who thinks that oral sex is just talking about it.

John B. Keane.

Referees are like wives, you can never tell how they're going to turn out.

John B. Keane.

Now listen lads, I'm not happy with our tackling. We're hurting them but they keep getting up.

John B. Keane ventures into coaching.

Keep your high balls low into the wind.

Advice to a young John B. Keane.

Micky Joe made his championship debut in such a way that he will never be asked to make it again.

John B. Keane.

Karl O'Dwyer will go down in history as the rat who joined the sinking ship.

Kerry fan on Karl's defection to Kildare.

AGRICULTURAL MATTERS

Brendan Kennelly was born in 1936 in Ballylongford. Although it has been a long time since he lived in Kerry there is one part of his native county that has never left him. Brendan had the dubious privilege of losing an All-Ireland minor final for Kerry in 1954! Well, kind of: referee Bill Jackson from Roscommon pulled him up for a foul on the left half-forward of the Dublin team, but Kennelly swears to God he never fouled him. The Dubs got a goal from it and then another goal from the kick-out. Kerry had been five points up with three minutes to go but Dublin got two goals and Brendan was the cause of the first one. Brendan claims that's been the cause of many a nightmare for him down the years. His memories are not those of the standard Kerry footballer:

> Mind games have long been part and parcel of football in Kerry as I discovered to my cost. As a boy in one of my first matches I found myself marking Pata Spring. I knew he was good and as he lined up at the half-way line before the throw-in to mark Pata I was really psyched up. Just before the ref threw in the ball Pata said, 'Do you know anything about sex?'
> I replied, 'I don't Pata.'
> 'Well I'll tell you about it now. It's like Kelly's bull and Sullivan's cow and that's how it happens and that's how you were born. Would you ever think about that now?'
> The ball was thrown in and I was left standing looking at Pata with my mouth open, pondering on the mysteries of the origins of life. It was a deliberate ploy to throw me. Pata was gone up the field with the ball while I was rooted to the spot burdened with the big questions of life.

THE MAN FROM VALENTIA

The most obvious reason for Kerry's success has been a phenomenal array of fantastic footballers from Dick Fitzgerald to Paddy Kennedy to 'Gooch' Cooper.

At the top of the footballing hierarchy in Kerry for John B. Keane was Mick O'Connell, reputed to have left the dressing room immediately after captaining Kerry to win the All-Ireland in 1959 and headed straight home for Kerry. Asked why he had to forgo the celebrations he is said to have replied, 'I had to go home to milk the cows.'

In emphasising O'Connell's ability to strike a ball John B. Keane told a story which showed how ecumenical his appeal was for both the sacred and the profane:

Mick was rowing from Valentia to the mainland and decided to practise his striking by taking a free from the boat. He hit it so hard that the ball burst on its journey. The cover of the ball landed outside the presbytery in Lisdoonvarna. The bladder landed outside a hoor house in Buenos Aires.

Ireland's finest sports writer Peter Woods has produced the most elegiac assessment of the man from Valentia:

I always remember seeing a television programme about the great Kerry footballer, Mick O'Connell. O'Connell used to run the roads of Valentia on his own. It was easy to tell he was well within himself: the camera showing him leaping upward and touching the branches of trees with his fingertips. Those branches were, I was well aware, far beyond the leap of any mortal. It would have been impossible not to have been impressed with the grace of O'Connell. To watch him, as a player, rise upward, field the ball and place a kick in a single fluid motion, like the half-seen dart of a deadly snake, so quickly that it might never have happened.

O'Connell is probably the most iconic name in gaelic football. However, he had an inner steel. Once, when knocked to the ground, an opponent said, 'Get up, you lazy f**ker.' O'Connell replied, 'You should catch a few balls while I'm down here because you'll catch no more when I get up.'

MR BIG

An apocryphal story told about the experiences of the Kerry team on tour illustrates a more generous side of their nature. The 'Bomber' Liston had many admirers, including one young lady from Australia, who engaged him in idle conversation. 'Excuse me, are you the Bomber?' asked an attractive, blonde Aussie. The Bomber nodded his assent. She responded with an obvious comment, 'You know you are one hell of a big man.' Again the Bomber nodded his head. As she barely reached his bellybutton, she gazed wistfully over his manly charms and asked, 'Are you all in proportion?'

He was forced to admit he was not. The light died in her eyes, only to be rekindled when he replied, 'If I was in proportion I'd be 6 ft 1 in.'

HAND ACTION

Long before Ger Loughnane came on the management scene Mick O'Dwyer was a great man to pull a stroke. In the late 1970s the Kerry team used the handpass a lot. At one point people started to complain that they weren't using it properly. Micko was concerned that it would cost the team dearly in an All-Ireland final if the players were penalised for not using it properly. So before the match he invited Paddy Collins, who was to be the referee for the big game to give them advice. Micko had each of his players doing all kinds of hand movements with the ball and every time he would ask: 'Is this okay Paddy?' Each time Collins would nod his head. When it came to the match the Kerry team did what they liked with the handpass because they knew Paddy Collins could not penalise them because he was the one who showed them how to use it.

SMALL TIME

Liam Griffin tells the story of how in 2002 he attended a social function with Dublin manager Tommy Lyons and Micko, who was still Kildare manager at the time. Tommy said to O'Dwyer at one stage, 'Micko, you and I will fill Croke Park this year.' O'Dwyer replied, "Tommy, you and I wouldn't fill a toilet!'

PILGRIMAGE

Mick O'Dwyer's wife was known to organise trips to Lourdes. One fan asked Micko: 'Did you ever go to Lourdes?'

The great man furrowed his brow and paused before inquiring: 'Did Kerry ever play there?'

THE BOSS

Tempora mutantur nos et mutamur in illis: Times change and we change with them.

One of the biggest changes in the world of the GAA over the last thirty years has been the prominence of the manager. It began in the 1970s with Kevin Heffernan and Mick O'Dwyer. Some people though wonder if there is a mercenary reason behind all this and recount the story of the rich GAA manager, the poor GAA manager and the tooth fairy who are in a room with a £100 pound note on the table when the lights go out. When the light comes back on the money is gone. So who took it? It's got to be the rich GAA manager because the other two are figments of the imagination.

Former GAA president Peter Quinn famously said: 'While there are many claims that managers are being paid under the table, the GAA couldn't even find the tables!'

Typically Pat Spillane has a view on this topic: 'In cases where there are paying managers the exact figures should be revealed. I know there is a fat chance of that happening. You have a better chance of seeing me beat Kylie Minogue in the competition for "Rear of the Year" than seeing any action on that front.'

In response to rumours that GAA managers were earning a small fortune Mick O'Dwyer replied: 'Ah sure, we're all going around with our arse out of our trousers.' O'Dwyer went further to explain his life of hardship: 'When I played we got a piece of orange at half-time, and if you were very quick you might get two.'

BON APPÉTIT

Pat Spillane is O'Dwyer's biggest champion. He is, though, known to poke fun at O'Dwyer's 'financial acumen': hence the story that every day he goes to a pub in Listowel for lunch. He always orders the soup of day. One day the manager asks him how he liked his meal. O'Dwyer replies, ''Twas good, but you could give a little more bread.'

So the next day the manager tells the waitress to give him four slices of bread. The manager asks him afterwards how he liked his meal. O'Dwyer replies, ''Twas good, but you could give a little more bread.'

So the next day the manager tells the waitress to give him eight slices of bread. 'How was your meal today, sir?' the manager asks. O'Dwyer replies, ''Twas good, but you could give a little more bread.'

The following day the manager tells the waitress to give him a whole loaf of bread with his soup. 'How was your meal, sir?' The manager asks when he comes to pay.

O'Dwyer replies, ''Twas good, but you could give a little more bread.'

The manager is now obsessed with seeing his famous customer say that he is satisfied with his meal, so he goes to the bakery, and orders a six-foot-long loaf of bread. When O'Dwyer comes in as usual the next day, the waitress and the manager cut the loaf in half, butter the entire length of each half, and lay it out along the counter, right next to his bowl of soup. O'Dwyer sits down, and devours both his bowl of soup, and both halves of the six-foot-long loaf of bread.

The manager now thinks he will get the answer he is looking for, and when O'Dwyer comes up to pay for his meal, the manager asks in his usual way: 'How was your meal *today*, sir?'

O'Dwyer replies: 'It was good as usual, but I see you've gone back to giving only two slices of bread.'

CRITICAL VOICES

Kerry are rightly seen as football royalty. However, in recent years Kerry people are often indignant about the comments of Joe Brolly in particular:

> On television you make a casual remark and people become suffused with rage. The odd time people will berate you for that. I recall travelling on a train to Dublin when a fella in a Meath jersey got up and said to me: 'You f**king boll*x.' During an ad break in the Wexford–Armagh quarter-final a man in his seventies burst into the studios and said to me: 'You're a f**king joke, yourself and O'Rourke. You're Dumb and Dumber.'
>
> I can say something relatively trivial and RTÉ gets a thousand emails. I said something about Paul Galvin after he kicked some one off the ball or something against Armagh in 2006. I said: 'That's unbelievable and he's a teacher. That's real corner-boy stuff.' Jesus Christ. All hell broke loose.

DEDICATED FOLLOWER OF FASHION

Off the field Paul Galvin is known as a fashion guru. On it he is known in part for the intensity of his jousts with Cork's Noel O'Leary. After O'Leary won an All-Ireland medal in 2010, Galvin sent him a text that read: 'Congrats on the win – now would you please f**k off and retire and leave me alone.'

THE CIRCLE OF LIFE

Success in gaelic football comes in cycles. Kerry are the un-disputed kings of gaelic football. In 2002 Kerry and Cork figured in a historic all-Munster All-Ireland semi-final the Kerry manager Páidí Ó Se asked for a home match for Kerry. Cork generously did not object so the match was played in Croke Park.

One of Ó Se's teammates in the glory days of the 1970s was Jimmy Deenihan. A bad injury caused Deenihan to retire prematurely but he went on to make a new career in politics. It was a bit of a cultural shock for him, particularly as he got some weird requests from his constituents. The strangest was the woman who asked him to see if he could arrange 'infidelity benefit' for herself and her husband.

However, even Kerry had their barren years. When he was president of the GAA Jack Boothman, at a time when Kerry football was in the doldrums before Maurice Fitzgerald brought them back to the Promised Land in 1997, went to the funeral of the legendary Paddy 'Bawn' Brosnan. Because of the pressures of time he was unable to make it to the church and went to meet the funeral at the graveyard. As he waited for the cortege to arrive he chatted with a few gravediggers. One of them gave a guided tour of the graveyard and pointed to the graves of all the famous footballers. It seemed that every second grave belonged to a former Kerry great. The gravedigger turned to Boothman and said, 'It's a very impressive collection isn't it.'

Boothman replied, ''Tis indeed but the way things are going you'll have to dig them up if Kerry are ever to win anything again!'

MONEY, MONEY, MONEY

Many Kerry folk believed they were cast-iron certainties to win the 1982 All-Ireland. A song to celebrate the victory had already been written. Then Offaly's super-sub Seamus Darby intervened with the winning goal and the Kingdom were deprived of history. Before the game a Kerry entrepreneur had invested a small fortune in making a large number of Kerry five-in-a-row t-shirts. His money would surely go to waste. Not a bit of it. With exceptional cunning, even by Kerry standards, he made an even bigger fortune by writing RIP on each of them and selling them all in Offaly.

CHAPTER FOUR

Hurlers on the Pitch and on the Ditch

Hurling is to Kilkenny what films are to Hollywood: a country-wide obsession that sets a pecking order, discussed endlessly and by everyone, complete with its own arcane laws and rituals. Pubs are the churches of this strange sporting religion. Hurling-talk is no idle form of gossip here, but a crucial element in the county's psyche, to which business, love, the land and the weather regularly take second place.

THE QUIET MAN

Kilkenny's Lorenzo Ignatius Meagher was perhaps the first true star of hurling. He was to hurling aficionados in the county what Nureyev was to the ballet enthusiast.

He won three All-Irelands in the 1930s and entered the club of GAA immortals on foot of his towering performance in dreadful weather in midfield when Kilkenny beat the hot favourites, and reigning champions, Limerick in the 1935 All-Ireland, having previously won All-Irelands in 1932 and 1933.

In Ireland we don't like players or personalities to get too big for the boots. This was best illustrated in the 1970s when someone said to Gay Byrne: 'There are no real stars in Ireland. You are the nearest thing we have to it but you are not there yet.'

Lory experienced this unique Irish trait when a fan approached him and said: 'You are a great forward. You always get great scores but you shoot the wides as well.'

He had a funeral fit for a prince when he died in 1973, such was his status within the game. For years young Kilkenny hurlers chanted 'Over the bar said Lory Meagher' when they scored in training sessions.

Apart from his genius on the field Meagher is renowned for his modesty off it. This character trait was most vividly illustrated when a journalist met him on the roadside one day and asked where he might track down Lory Meagher. The Kilkenny ace's reply was: 'You've just missed him. He passed up this way a few minutes ago. If you hurry you've a good chance of catching him.'

BEAUTY SLEEP

In 1966 Kilkenny lost the All-Ireland to Cork although they were red-hot favourites. Cork won by 3–9 to 1–10. The papers the next day were full of talk about 'the year of the sleeping pill'. It was the first year players had taken them before an All-Ireland final. There was a lot of smart comments afterwards that the Kilkenny players took them too late because they hadn't fully woken up until after the match!

DEDICATED FAN

In 1979 after Kilkenny beat Galway in the All-Ireland hurling final Fan Larkin rushed off the field into the dressing room to change. A clearly startled Mick Dunne went into the Kilkenny room just minutes after the match to prepare later for a live interview only to see Fan already fully clothed. Clearly Fan had missed the presentation. Dunne asked him why he was in the dressing room so quickly?

'I have to go to Mass Mick,' replied Fan matter-of-factly.

CHICKS WITH STICKS

Camogie's most famous star is Kilkenny's Angela Downey. During an All-Ireland final Angela was goal bound when her opponent made a despairing lunge at her which caused Angela's skirt to end up on the ground. Undeterred, Angela kept on running, smashed the ball into the net and then calmly returned to collect her skirt.

DIVINE FAVOUR

In the beginning, God and DJ Carey were seen as quite separate individuals. It was only later confusion crept in.

One story illustrates DJ's status in the game: the All-Heaven hurling final was taking place between Kilkenny and Tipperary. The Tipperary team were powered by some of the giants of deceased hurlers. The Kilkenny team likewise had the pick of players from their county who had gone on to their eternal reward and were captained by Ollie Walsh. With just three minutes to go Tipperary were leading by three goals and two points. Suddenly there was a gasp from the crowd as a sub appeared on the Kilkenny team wearing the number fourteen jersey. In the final three minutes four balls were pumped into the square. The super-sub got the four of them and stuck each of them in the net. The Cats won by a point. After the game was over St Peter went over to commiserate with the Tipperary stars. The Tipp players were stunned by the appearance of the sub and asked, 'I never knew DJ Carey died. When did it happen?'

St Peter replied, 'Oh that's not DJ. That's God. He just thinks he's DJ Carey.'

THE BITTER WORD

Mind you, a prophet is not always appreciated in his own land. In 1997 before Clare played Kilkenny in the All-Ireland semi-final

Ger Loughnane was asked in an interview what he thought of DJ. He had been absolutely brilliant in the All-Ireland quarter-final in a thrilling game against Galway in Thurles. He practically beat the Westerners all on his own. Loughnane said:

> DJ will prove himself to be an outstanding player when he plays really well against one of the best players in the country in a big match. Next Sunday he will be playing in a really big match against Brian Lohan and if he plays really well against Brian, he will prove himself to be a really great player but I won't regard him as a great player until he does it against somebody like Brian on the big day.

Nicky Brennan was Kilkenny manager then and he taped the interview and played it on the bus on the way to the match. According to folklore Nicky said, 'Listen to what that c**t Loughnane said about one of our best players.' Legend has it that Eddie O'Connor is supposed to have piped up, 'He's f**king right!'

TOP OF THE WORLD

One of hurling's great evangelists is Liam Griffin, former Wexford manager. Griffin brought a new professionalism to the job and a lot of new practices. At one of his first meetings with the panel Griffin gave them a questionnaire to fill out. It had a number of questions such as 'Where would you prefer to train?' At the bottom was an additional query, 'What is your favourite position?' Most players answered in the obvious way – full-back, half-back, full-forward, etc. The exception was the joker from Faythe Harriers, Larry O'Gorman, who gave Griffin information he didn't really need. His reply was simply, 'On Top!'

MANLY MEN

Hurling is a man's game. One of few hurlers who have starred for two counties was Jim Fives who played for both Waterford and Galway. Fives glows affectionately as he recalls some of the more unusual incidents in his career, with the wonder of a baby counting his toes. At one stage he was playing a junior hurling match for Tourin against Ballyduff in Lismore. His full-forward 'manhandled' their goalie and a melee developed around the goal because they tried to lynch him and he ran. Everyone got involved. What made it unusual was that all thirty players ended up against the railing of the pitch first and then things got so hot and heavy that they all ended up in the next field. As the faction-fighting was at its height someone remarked, 'Come here for a laugh and you'll go home in stitches.'

TUFF STUFF

People who are the most meek and mild in normal life can be transformed once they get on the hurling field. Former Antrim star Sambo McNaughton famously recalled marking Fr Iggy Clarke on his inter-county debut, 'My innocent childhood perception of the priesthood changed after that game!'

HALL OF FAME

Hurling fans down through the years have been inspired by their heroes to produce a number of classic comments:

Carlos Santana.
> *The nickname given by Carlton Australian Rules club fans to Setanta Ó hAilpín. The Cork version is simply 'Santy'.*

The lion and the lamb shall lie down together, but the lamb won't get much sleep.

Clare fan on any opponent facing up to Brian Lohan.

I didn't get Christy Ring's autograph, but he trod on my toe though.

Cork fan.

Everyone knows which come first when it's a question of hurling or sex – all discerning people recognise that.

Tipperary fan.

Funny game hurling, especially the way Kerry play it.

Cork fan.

To be a great goalie, you need a big heart, big hands and a big bottom.

Comment about a former Antrim goalie.

The man from Del Monte said yes.

*Delighted Kilkenny fan
after DJ Carey reverses his initial decision to retire.*

Pessimists see a cup that is half-empty. Optimists see a cup that is half-full. But we haven't even seen the cup.

Sligo hurling fan.

Jesus saves – but Jimmy Barry-Murphy scores on the rebound.

Graffiti.

I love Cork so much that if I caught one of their hurlers in bed with my missus I'd tiptoe downstairs and make him a cup of tea.

Joe Lynch.

He [Nicky English] spoilt the game – he got too many scores.

Antrim fan at the 1989 All-Ireland.

When Sylvie Linnane is good, he's great. When he's bad he's better!

Galway fan.

It's all over ... Clare are ... Jeeesus.

Matthew McMahon Clare FM GAA commentator reacting to Clare's Munster final triumph in 1995.

The cigarettes are being lit here in the commentary box, the lads are getting anxious, it's a line ball down there to Clare and who's going to take it ... Will ye put them out lads yee'll choke me.

Matthew McMahon during the 1995 All-Ireland final.

Quirke-y

Carlow's dual star Paddy Quirke played senior football and hurling with the county in the 1970s and 1980s. He also played hurling in San Francisco and found it really tough and physical. At one stage he put in his hurley, angled with the bas to the ground, to block an opponent; got a severe belt across the face and was taken off and rushed to hospital. He had no social security cover, but his friends who were with him decided he was Patrick Foley (a genuine holder of social security). So all of a sudden he was somebody else. The only problem was when Paddy heard the name Patrick Foley being called out in the hospital he forgot that was supposed to be him and had to be reminded who he then was.

At that stage he was not in very good shape and was expecting some sympathy from the doctor. Instead all he said was, 'Were you playing that crazy Irish game?'

HARE-RAISING

In 1985 Paddy played for his club Naomh Eoin against the Westmeath champions Brownstown in the first round of the Leinster club hurling championship. One of his teammates was asked a few days later how bad the pitch was. He replied, 'Well the grass was so long a hare rose at half-time!'

HURLERS ON THE PITCH AND ON THE DITCH

Hurling is the greatest game because of the thrills and spills on the pitch and the level of analysis off it. Like their footballing counterparts, hurlers have made some memorable comments. What follows is a collection of classic hurling quotes:

Those guys in the media who wrote off Cork in the winter must have spent all their time watching Coronation Street.

> *Cork midfielder Jerry O'Connor*
> *responding to Cork's easy win over Clare in 2007.*

You should play every game as if it's your last, but make sure you perform well enough to ensure it's not.

> *Jack Lynch.*

It's hard to see the writing on the wall when your back is up against it.

> *Seán Óg Ó hAilpín on the 2006 All-Ireland defeat to Kilkenny.*

Cork are like the mushrooms; they can come overnight.

> *Jim 'Tough' Barry.*

Hurling: it's all a matter of inches – those between your ears.

> *Antrim's Kevin Armstrong.*

Hurling and sex are the only two things you can enjoy without being good at it.

Jimmy Deane.

Broken marriages, conflicts of loyalty, the problems of everyday life fall away as one faces up to DJ Carey.

Wexford player.

I said to the manager, this is supposed to be a five-star hotel and there's a bloody hole in the roof. He turned around and said, 'That's where you can see the five stars from.'

Paddy Quirke on All-Stars tour.

A fan is a person who, when you have made an idiot of yourself on the pitch, doesn't think you've done a permanent job.

Jack Lynch.

A referee should be a man. They are, for the most part, old women.

Nicky Rackard.

They haven't come to see you umpiring, they have come to see me hurl.

Christy Ring after a clash with an umpire.

I think they can improve on their 100% record.

Brian Whelahan.

If Eoin's shot had gone in, it would have been a goal.

Tony Browne.

I am a firm believer that you have to score more than the other team if you want to win.

Henry Shefflin.

If a team scores early on, it often takes an early lead.

DJ Carey.

You cannot possibly have counted the number of passes Kilkenny made, but there were eight.

Tomás Mulcahy.

Ah sure, Daly you can't score a point and what's worse you can't f**king even pull a pint!

Limerick fan after Anthony Daly
(publican and legendary Clare player) missed a long-range free.

OFFALY SERIOUS

Offaly's Pat Carroll was known for his dedication to hurling as revealed in the following conversation:

Pat: My hurley was stolen this morning.
Friend: That's terrible – where did you lose it?
Pat: In the car park.
Friend: Did the thieves damage your car?
Pat: I don't know, they stole that too!

HEALTH AND SAFETY

The Munster final replay in 1998 between Waterford and Clare had probably the most 'physically robust' opening to a game in GAA history. There's a story told about the two grasshoppers who came onto the field before the game.

As the pulling started between the players on both teams, one said to the other, 'We're going to be killed here today. Do you feel the tension?'

The other replied, 'I do. Hop up here on the sliotar. It's the only place we'll be safe!'

A Good Walk Spoiled

After retirement many former GAA stars turn to golf. Waterford's erstwhile hurling All-Star Paul Flynn went so far as to compete in the West of Ireland amateur championship at Rosses Point when Ireland had a white Easter in 2013. In the arctic conditions Flynn struggled and scored an opening round of eighty-three. When asked if the experience was tougher than facing Kilkenny in an All-Ireland final the former sharpshooter stoically replied: 'It was a slower death anyway.'

The Clash of the Ash

Disappointingly Flynn only found himself on the subs bench when Waterford reached the All-Ireland only for the Déise to be humiliated in a twenty-three point defeat. Before the match Kilkenny's Christy Heffernan was asked if he thought the Waterford players would be fit enough. He replied: 'They should be fit enough, they've been training for forty-five years!'

Since his retirement in 2008 Flynn has become a pundit on *The Sunday Game*. As a pundit Flynn has raised eyebrows himself when he was critical of Davy Fitzgerald's management of the Waterford team, particularly of the type of drills done in training. While acknowledging that Flynn was one of the greatest hurlers of modern times Davy's riposte was that while the training was 'up to speed I am not sure Paul Flynn was'.

Dan the Man

Flynn leaves the game with many happy memories of his former teammates. A case in point is Dan Shanahan, an employee of Top Oil, who went into a shop one day in 2007. At that stage he had become hurling's supreme goal machine – he had just starred in Waterford's triumph over Cork in the All-Ireland hurling quarter-final and had scored eight goals and eight points in his four games that year, bringing his championship score from 2004 to an incredible nineteen goals and thirty-six points.

A little lady of mature years eyed him up slowly. Suddenly a smile of triumph came over her face. 'I know who you are now,' said the woman.

'That's good,' said Big Dan politely.

'You're the oil man!' the woman replied with a flourish.

BACK DOOR

After Offaly lost the Leinster final in 1998 to Kilkenny their manager Babs Keating met with the County Board and decided to stay but the next morning he resigned because he was 'shocked' by an interview in a newspaper with Offaly's star midfielder Johnny Pilkington who had questioned his record with the county, stating that Babs had abandoned Offaly's tradition of ground hurling and questioning the tactics against Kilkenny. Michael Bond replaced Babs and they went on to win the All-Ireland that year.

Broadcaster Peter Woods offers an interesting perspective on Offaly's revived fortunes under Michael Bond: 'You could lead them with a thread but you can't drive them with an iron bar.'

Hubert Ringey, the Offaly captain, in his victory speech after Offaly beat Kilkenny in the All-Ireland final said: 'We might have come in the back door, but we're going out the front door.' Offaly came through the back door, having voted against it and Offaly, true to form, voted against the back door the following year.

THE PLAYBOY OF THE SOUTHERN WORLD

'Nothing is permanent except change.' So said Heraclitus, Greek philosopher in 500 BC.

The world of gaelic games is constantly evolving and changing but the one constant is that each generation produces its own legends and iconic names. Limerick's Mick Mackey was both an extraordinary hurler and a great character. He had an immense physical and social presence. Few people could match him for charisma.

Nicknames are not generally part of the culture in the GAA, unlike rugby. There is no question that this is a good thing. There have been a few exceptions like Antrim manager Liam Bradley who is known as 'baker' because back in the 1970s he always wore a white sports jacket. What makes Mick Mackey unique among the giants of gaelic games was that he had three nicknames. He was often described as 'The Laughing Cavalier', occasionally as 'King of the Solo Run' but most often as 'The Playboy of the Southern World'. He always seemed to have a smile on his face – both on and off the field. He was one of those exceptional talents who made the crowd come alive because of his swashbuckling style and the higher the stakes the better he performed, which is a sure sign of greatness.

HURLERS OFF THE PITCH

Hurling managers down through the years have been known to produce and inspire some magnificent moments:

Ger Loughnane isn't here today, which strongly suggests he might be somewhere else.

Cyril Farrell.

There are guys up there on the Council and *change*? They couldn't even spell the word.

Eamon Cregan on the Central Council.

Never watch a gaelic football match before hurling as it slows the mental reflexes.

Mentor to Cork team in the 1960s.

I have never seen an organisation so hidebound by bullsh*t.

Liam Griffin on the GAA.

And as for you. You're not even good enough to play for this shower of useless no-hopers.

Former Clare mentor to one of his subs after a heavy defeat.

Well, it's Clare 1–14 and Wexford 0–8, and if the score stays this way, I've got to fancy Clare for the win.

Liam Griffin.

He had an eternity to play that ball, but took too long.

Liam Griffin.

Knowing what goes on in Justin McCarthy's head is a bigger mystery than the third secret of Fatima.

Waterford fan.

Loughnane had us coming out of that dressing room with smoke coming out of our backsides.

Anthony Daly on the build-up to a Munster final against Cork.

Hurlers do not stop playing because they grow old; they grow old because they stop playing.

Liam Griffin.

They look like world beaters going forward and panel beaters in the defence.

Cyril Farrell on Galway in 2005.

That could have made it a five-point-lead and there's a subtle difference between that and four points.

Cyril Farrell.

An ounce of breeding is worth a tonne of feeding.

> *Former Clare boss Tony Considine*
> *reflecting on the introduction of Barry Loughnane,*
> *Ger's son, against Laois in the 2007 qualifiers.*

MISSED OPPORTUNITIES

As Waterford manager, Justin McCarthy was less than impressed by a fringe player with the team. He said to him, 'It's a pity you didn't take up the game sooner.'

'You mean I'd be better now?'

'No, you would have given up the game long ago.'

CHIN UP

Hurlers bring their own unique personalities to acceptance speeches. After captaining Wexford to a rare Leinster under-21 title in 2013 their captain Lee Chin, began his speech: '*An bhfuil cead agam dul go dti an leithreas?* That's the only Irish I know.'

HELP ME IF YOU CAN I'M FEELING DOWN

At the start of the 2013 hurling championship the favourites were Kilkenny and Tipperary. After Tipperary lost very early in the qualifiers and Cork beat Kilkenny in the quarter-finals a request was made to stage the All-Ireland hurling semi-finals in Semple Stadium (Tipperary) and Nowlan Park (Kilkenny). Why? To support hurling in the weaker counties, of course.

CHAPTER FIVE

The Men from Clare

It is sometimes said that Ger Loughnane is a perfectionist. A perfectionist is one who takes great pains – and gives them to everyone else!

I suppose a lot of people would also describe him as hurling's answer to José Mourinho. That is rubbish. Given that Feakle's second most famous person, behind Biddy Early, was annoying officials and giving out about referees long before 'the Special One' it is much more accurate to say that José, in his amazing monocoloured overcoat, is soccer's answer to Ger Loughnane.

Former Liverpool manager, Bill Shankly, said of his full-back, Tommy Smith, that he would raise an argument in a graveyard. With commendable honesty Loughnane says that the same comment could be made about himself.

Ger brought some of the qualities he showed as a player to his job as a coach. In the 1976 League final replay Eddie Keher got a head injury and the blood was pumping out of him necessitating a long delay while he got attention. Loughnane, ever helpful and compassionate, went up to him and said, 'Jaysus Keher, would you ever get up and get on with it. Sure there's nothing wrong with you!'

GOING DUTCH

As a player Loughnane won two All-Star awards and two National League medals. As a result of their success in the late 1970s the Clare team were invited by a hockey team called 'the hurling club' to play an exhibition game against Wexford in Holland to mark the club's centenary. The hosts took the hurlers to the Heineken factory in Amsterdam and were amazed at the gusto by which the Irish delegation attacked the free samples.

The match itself took place on a manicured lawn in Amsterdam. After the game the Clare team somehow ended up in a bar in a seedy back lane in Amsterdam's red-light district. Much later on into the night Loughnane noticed one of his teammates leaving the bar, very much the worse for wear. Loughnane left to see his friend stumbling into a dark alley, which was obviously very dangerous. As Loughnane went to escort him to safety he was greeted by the question, 'Is this f**king O'Connell street?' The other player thought he was in Ennis!

PRIMITIVE

Loughnane had a stormy relationship with officials, including those in Clare. Among their number was Brendan Vaughan, the former chairman of the County Board. Both are teachers and once at a schoolboy match between their two schools they nearly came to blows. There were two coats down as goalposts. There was no crossbar. Vaughan was umpire at one side. Loughnane was umpire at the other. A head-high ball came in at one stage. Vaughan said it was a goal. Loughnane said it was a point. After a full and frank exchange of views Vaughan looked at Loughnane disdainfully and uttered the immortal words, 'Get away, you bushman from Feakle.'

VAN THE MAN

In 1995 the Clare team went to Thurles to train on the pitch ten days before the Munster final. The man who normally supplied food to the team after training gave them his van to take food down to Thurles. Loughnane volunteered to take the van, which may not be the cleverest idea as he had never driven a van before. He had his son, Barry, with him and they were to pick up Frank Lohan on the way. They came to a T-junction and he could not find the brake without looking down. There was a woman crossing the road. Loughnane went right across the road, barely avoiding the woman, and just before hitting the footpath he managed to turn the van around. Then he was able to look down and see where the brake was. They collected Frank and put Barry in the back of the van which was nothing but a freezer, because all the food was frozen. When they got to Tipperary town they stopped because it was so hot and they decided to get a cool drink. Loughnane went back and opened the door for Barry. He was nearly frozen alive.

FRIENDLY CHAT

During his time as Clare manager Loughnane was not always very popular with Tipperary fans. After Clare beat Tipperary in the replay in the 1999 Munster championship Tony Considine and Loughnane decided they would walk into Cork city from Pairc Uí Chaoimh. It was about three quarters of an hour after the game. The crowd had dispersed. They were walking along and they saw a van up ahead of them with a Tipperary registration. When they were about twenty yards away from them the driver spotted them and jumped out of the van. Loughnane said to Tony, 'Here's trouble.'

The driver said, 'Howya Ger? Any chance of the autograph?'

Loughnane was relieved that he wasn't going to attack him. He told him no problem and as the driver handed him the programme to sign he told Ger it was for his wife. He wrote, 'To Marion. Best wishes, Ger Loughnane.' The driver never looked up at him but turned to his friend and said, 'Jesus Johnny she'll get some surprise when she goes home this evening. Christ, wait till she sees this.'

Then he turned to Loughnane and said, 'You have no idea how much she hates you!'

GUESS WHO

Despite Loughnane's happy capacity for weathering hostility, the strains that had been mounting mercilessly over the years as manager took their toll. The biggest casualty was his hairline. At the peak of the Clare team's success there was a table quiz in Shannon. For one of the rounds, they showed pictures of well-known people when they were young. A photo of Loughnane was included from back in the days when he had really long hair. When one of the teams were asked to identify his photo they answered, 'Princess Diana!'

POWER TO ALL OUR FRIENDS

After he stepped down as manager of the Clare team, there were strong rumours that Loughnane would be interested in getting involved in politics. Subsequently he was courted by two political parties. Loughnane's mischievous streak may have been a contributory factor to this round of speculation. In 1999 he agreed to a request from Clare FM to take part in an April Fool's Day joke. The local elections were coming up at the time, so he announced on Clare FM that he was resigning from the Clare team and was going to stand for the County Council. He stated that there were things more important than hurling and that he was going to stand as an independent, and that a lot of the Clare team were going to campaign for him. He launched into a passionate tirade about the need to improve the roads in East Clare. So convincing was he that many people swallowed the story hook, line and sinker and the station was inundated with phone calls. Such was the reaction that the station had to issue a statement that evening to admit that it was all a joke.

MEDIA MANAGEMENT

Throughout his management career Loughnane was called a lot of things but one person he was never compared with was Mother Teresa. Yet they had one thing in common: Mother Teresa famously said, 'Facing the press is more difficult than bathing a leper.' During his tenure as Clare manager, Loughnane had a stormy relationship with the media. Before the 1995 All-Ireland final he said of his media interviews, 'I say nothing but I never stop talking.'

WINING AND DINING

In 2002 Loughnane was having a quiet meal with his wife, Mary, in a restaurant in Ennis. Out of the corner of his eye he noticed the *Sunday Tribune's* then hurling correspondent, Enda McEvoy, entering the restaurant. A natural born mischief-maker, Loughnane dispatched his wife Mary to make contact. Enda was hardly seated when Mary approached him and said with Nicole Kidman-like acting skills, 'I'm very sorry sir I'm going to have to ask you to leave.'

Enda was gobsmacked. 'What do you mean?'

'Well sir the last time you were here you were caught on video camera leaving after your meal without paying your bill.'

McEvoy was stunned, 'But … but … but I've never been here before.'

A pantomime developed with an exchange on the lines of 'Oh yes you did … Oh no I didn't.' The journalist could not believe he was being accused of such an offence and was getting increasingly bewildered and distressed. Eventually he heard the loud laughter coming from another table and turned around to see Loughnane splitting his sides laughing.

WISH YOU WERE HERE

My favourite story about Ger though is that after Clare won the All-Ireland in 1995 he went to the travel agent and said: 'We've won the All-Ireland, our first victory in the final for eighty-one years. We've plenty of money raised, we can go anywhere in the world. I've only one stipulation. We need to go somewhere where nobody knows anything about hurling.'

The travel agent replied: 'Sir, you have two choices: Thailand or Tipperary.'

THE STRIFE OF BRIAN

Loughnane attracts strong opinions. In 2001 I worked with him on a modest publication about his life, which showcased his characteristic reserve and understatement. One of my most vivid memories from that fascinating experience was asking him to write a pen-picture of each of the players on his Clare team. A few weeks later he handed me five foolscap pages with notes on each player from one to fifteen. Those five pages would make very interesting reading for many people in Clare but are locked away deep in a vault in a bank in Geneva. What struck me was the one that stood out visually from all the others. Underneath Brian Lohan's name were just three words in block letters:

SIMPLY THE BEST

Four years later on a frosty February evening in Ennis I had the honour of meeting Brian, the best full-back I have ever seen, and I asked him: 'What was Loughnane like?' I was curious if he would reciprocate the compliment. He furrowed his brow for a moment and then he summed up his former manager with four immortal words: 'Loughnane was a brute!'

ARE WE THERE YET?

Loughnane is known for his capacity to talk. One evening in the difficult year of 1998 he and Tony Considine were driving home late from a training session in Flannans. As the road was very frosty Considine was been very careful to drive safely. After he drove about ten miles a garda pulled Considine over and said: 'Sir, do you realise your passenger fell out of the car five miles back?'

To which Considine replied: 'Thank God, I thought I had gone deaf.'

RAISING THE BANNER

There are so many words Loughnane has generated down the years. The following are my personal favourites:

Dying is easy. Winning a Munster final is hard.
Loughnane after Clare end sixty-three years in the wilderness in 1995.

A Munster final is not a funeral, though both can be very sad affairs.

I felt sicker than a pilgrim in Lourdes.
Loughnane on 'the Colin Lynch affair' in 1998.

Even Mother Teresa wouldn't support us.
Loughnane on the same saga.

We've got grounds which are state of the art and administration which is state of the Ark.

A dig at the Munster Council.

He had a photographic memory that was never developed.

Loughnane on a Munster Council official in 1998.

People say I am mad but I prefer to think of myself as open to unconventional thinking.

Loughnane on his unorthodox selection policy.

I am sorry if I caused offence by comparing the Muster Council to donkeys. I wish to unreservedly apologise to the donkeys.

Loughnane after the controversies of 1998.

I'm not giving away any secrets like that to Tipperary. If I had my way, I wouldn't even tell them the time of the throw-in.

Loughnane on his controversial selection policy.

What does posterity need me for? Nothing. But what would I like said about me at my funeral? I'd like someone to say, 'Look! He's moving!'

The Golden Days are Over

When Loughnane became Galway coach in 2006 the Cats fans told the story of the Clare hurling fan who was walking through the streets of Ennis when he saw a sale on at a video shop. When he stopped to look he saw a video called *Clare Hurling: The Golden Years.* The guy entered the shop and asked how much the video cost. Given an answer, he replied in shock, 'What! I'm not paying €300 just for a video!' The shop owner replied, 'No don't be silly, the video is €5 the Betamax video player is €295.'

BLESS ME FATHER

Loughnane also famously antagonised one or two high-profile clergy in Clare in 1998 with his account of a conversation between them which was overheard in Croke Park.

A lorry driver who was also a Tipperary fan, was heading down the Ennis road when he saw a priest at the side of the road. Feeling it was his duty, he stopped to give the priest a lift. A short time later, he saw Loughnane on the side of the road and aimed his lorry at him. At the last second, he thought of the priest with him and realised he couldn't run over the hurling manager, so he swerved, but he heard a thump anyway. Looking back as he drove on, he didn't see anything. He began to apologise for his behaviour to the priest. I'm sorry, Father. I barely missed that f**k … that fella at the side of the road.'

But the priest said, 'Don't worry, son. I got him with my door.'

RADIO GA GA

In 1998 Loughnane famously went to war with the Munster Council in an explosive interview with Clare FM. In fact he was so cheesed off by the whole affair that he decided to get away from it all and go for a holiday in the sun. At one stage to get a break from the beach he went into a hi-tech electrical store to buy a car radio and the salesman said, 'This is the very latest model. It's voice-activated. You just tell it what you want to listen to and the station changes automatically. There's no need to take your hands off the wheel.'

When he returned to Ireland he had it installed and the first morning as he was driving to school he decided to test it. He said 'Pop' and the sound of the Beatles filled the car. He said 'Country' and instantly he was listening to Daniel O'Donnell. Then suddenly two pedestrians stepped off the pavement in front of him, causing him to swerve violently and shout 'F**king idiots!' at them. Then the radio changed to a documentary on the Munster Council.

THE PEOPLE HAVE SPOKEN

Some of the classic 'anti-Loughnane' comments include:

Ger Loughnane is paranoid. He's the Woody Allen of hurling.

Tipperary fan.

There's only one head bigger than Ger Loughnane's and that's Birkenhead.

Limerick fan.

He cost Irish industry £25 million because workers were talking about Ger Loughnane when they should have been doing their jobs!

Clare fan after the famous Loughnane interview on Clare FM at the height of the Colin Lynch controversy.

It would be easier if he was trying to sell Eircom shares.

Clare fan on Cyril Lyons's task of succeeding Loughnane as Clare manager.

Ger Loughnane was fair, he treated us all the same during training – like dogs.

Clare player.

Ger Loughnane should be made Minister for the Environment given his contribution to gas emissions.

Ivan Yates.

KNOCK, KNOCK, KNOCKING ON HEAVEN'S DOOR

There are many apocryphal stories about Loughnane, though few are printable. One deals with the day he faced God at the throne of heaven with Christy Ring and Mick Mackey. God said to them, 'Before granting you a place at my side, I must ask for your beliefs.'

Ring stared God directly in the eye and said, 'I believe hurling is the meaning of life. Nothing else has brought so much joy to so many. I have devoted my life to spreading the gospel of hurling.'

God was moved by his passion and eloquence and said, 'You are a man of true faith. Sit by me at my right hand.'

He then turned to Limerick's most famous hurling son, 'Now, my child tell me what you believe in?'

'I believe courage, bravery, loyalty, teamwork, dedication and commitment are the soul of life and I dedicated my career to living up to those ideals.'

God replied, 'You have spoken well my child. Sit by me at my left hand.'

Then he turned to Loughnane, 'And you, Mr Loughnane, what is that you believe?'

Loughnane gave him the withering look that he usually reserved for referees and members of the Munster Council and replied, 'I believe that you are sitting in my chair.'

INTO THE WEST

In 2006 Loughnane began an unsuccessful two years as Galway manager, where he had a jaundiced view both of some of the county's hurling officials and the training facilities:

I was on the Hurling Development Committee, which tried to persuade Galway to come into the Leinster championship. When we met them, one official fell asleep at the end of the table. That's a fact. Another official's only concern was that the kitchen was closing at 9 p.m., so the meeting had to be over then, so that he'd get his meal. They weren't the slightest bit interested.

Ballinasloe is like a sheep field. Loughrea is an absolute disgrace – a tiny cabbage garden of a field. Athenry is the worst of all. I asked myself what were these people doing in the 1980s when they had all this success? It was Pearse Stadium they concentrated on – the stand, not the pitch. Because the pitch is like something left over from Famine times, there are so many ridges in it.

BACK TO BASICS

Clare started training for the 1995 Munster championship the previous September. Clare trained all the way through the League. Luxurious conditions were not conducive to good winter training so they trained in Crusheen. Mike McNamara was excellent for putting the players through that hard physical slog. The players will never forget their introduction to Mike's training methods and personality. On his very first night standing on the pitch in Crusheen he said, 'Okay ladies. Let's go for a jog.'

DANCING QUEENS

In the noughties Armagh and Tyrone pioneered a new style of defensive football and were seen as trailblazers for the other counties to follow. This was not seen as part of the natural order by the purists, in Kerry in particular. Twice All-Ireland winning captain Anthony Daly recalls meeting Tomás Ó Sé and the Kerry defender said: 'I'm sick of that Northern crowd. If they went set dancing twice a week, we'd all be set dancing twice a week.'

Let Me Entertain You

During a game communication is almost impossible on the field because of the noise. Loughnane had to rely on his players for leadership on the field. Anthony Daly was the natural choice to be the team's spokesman and captain. As a player he deserved all the plaudits heaped upon him with a string of performances as captivating as the sport can offer. Daly had to be what he was, an excellent craftsman with a superb fighting spirit and the stamina of body and mind to cope with the long haul. While his famous speeches and innate media skills might have seemed to be his obvious credentials, Loughnane chose him for his ability in the dressing room, given his flair to help players cope with frustration and disappointment. 'Dalo' was adept at deflecting any anger by giving his teammates a chance to air their complaints.

Never was Daly's role as captain more clearly illustrated than during the Munster final in 1995:

> The scenes when we won the Munster final in 1995 were something to treasure. You have to remember that when people talked about winning in Clare all they meant was winning the Munster final. The All-Ireland final wasn't even contemplated because the Munster final had always been such a stumbling block.
>
> For myself personally it was winning the Munster final and the satisfaction out of that. The boys often talk about how unprepared the Clare people were for our win. We got back to Clarecastle and there was no podium. I had to stand on the top of the bus. My mother was an avid Bingo goer to Ennis on Sunday nights and all I said was it must be a very special night when my mother wasn't gone to bingo.

Dalo's popularity is such that he is even respected in Cork. After his Dublin team controversially lost a thriller to Cork in the 2013 All-Ireland semi-final the Cork fans website featured a new posting: 'Clareman and Dublin bainisteoir Anthony Daly, is also an annoyingly likeable character which is in stark contrast to the less palatable contemporary managing his home county.'

WHAT IT SAYS IN THE PAPERS

The former president of the Camogie Association is Liz Howard, best known for years as a pundit on *The Sunday Game*. Liz became embroiled in a major controversy following Clare's victory in the epic Munster final in 1997. Anthony Daly made a speech in which he articulated the feelings and motivations of all Clare players and supporters on that day. Daly had that uncanny knack of putting into words exactly what every Clare person was feeling and his comment 'We're no longer the whipping boys of Munster' captured perfectly the mood of the day. A massive cheer went up from the Clare supporters when he uttered these words.

To the utter consternation of everyone in Clare Liz Howard, then the PRO of the Tipperary County Board, wrote in a newspaper article that the statement was 'conduct unbecoming'. Liz spent most of her youth living in Feakle, where her father was the local sergeant, so her comments hit a nerve, especially in her former home village.

However, when she repeated this 'conduct unbecoming' theme two weeks later, the whole thing spiralled out of control. Other newspapers picked it up and it became the topic of conversation. Ger Loughnane wrote an open letter to Liz Howard and that's when the whole controversy really took off.

It finally spawned an amusing sequel when a man came to the door of Daly's shop in Ennis and said, 'You shouldn't have said that.'

Daly replied, 'What did I say?'

'Well, I don't know. But you shouldn't have said it.'

From Clare To Here

In 1999 Eamon Cregan listed former Clare hurler Jimmy Smyth as one of the top five hurlers of the twentieth century. The same year Jimmy was presented with an award as Clare person of the year. In his acceptance speech Jimmy remembered a story his uncle used to relate regarding a man who could not get out of bed in the morning and who made a firm resolution that this would be rectified. He employed the services of his landlady to act as his alarm clock and she assured him that in the future he would be called at 8 a.m. sharp. His friends heard of this resolve and blackened the man's face with shoe polish when he was asleep. The landlady was true to her word and called him promptly at 8 a.m. He got up immediately, looked at his face in the mirror and said, 'Good God, 'twas the wrong man she called' and jumped back into bed again.

Come On Christy

Throughout his career Smyth came across many characters. The goalkeeper on his club team, Christy Jones, had a great puck-out. Back then the sliotar was much heavier than it is today. They both grew up in Ruan, which is about six miles from Ennis and eight miles from Doora. Doora might as well have been South Africa because it was too long a distance for them to travel at a time when no one had a car. Jimmy asked Christy once what was the greatest puck-out he had ever struck. He answered, 'If I had the ball they have today I'd drive it to f**king Doora.'

Be Calm

There was a man in Ruan who was a great admirer of Jimmy's. One day he was bearing down on goal in a very tense match and the harder he ran the more the Ruan crowd was getting excited. Everyone was giving him advice and he could hear all kinds of suggestions about what he should do. Then, just as he was trying to concentrate, he heard his number-one fan roaring out over the din, 'Take no notice of them, Jimmy, make your own arrangements.'

However, Smyth had not always such a happy relationship with priests on the hurling field. He was playing a club match one day when a fracas developed and most of the crowd invaded the pitch. A priest was among them and he had a few choice words for Jimmy; but Jimmy simply said, 'Father, you should be on the sideline giving good example to the young.' The next day the priest's mother came to visit Smyth and thanked him for the good advice he had given her son.

IT COULD HAPPEN TO A BISHOP

One of the things that always struck the former Bishop of Killaloe, Willie Walsh, about hurling was the strange way positional switches were made in a match, particularly in the 1990 hurling final between Cork and Galway. After about fifteen minutes he was wondering what the Cork selectors were going to do about Jim Cashman. Joe Cooney was destroying him and he couldn't understand why they left Jim there. They went in at half-time and Bishop Willie said in the stands, 'Well Jim Cashman won't be centre-back in the second half' but amazingly he was and he went on to win his battle with Joe Cooney in the second half and Cork won the All-Ireland.

When Bishop Walsh went back to Clare some people said to him, 'Ah, you can't beat those Cork guys. Now if that was Clare we'd have panicked and taken Jim Cashman off but the Cork guys were wise and knew what was best.' Of course that was a bit hurtful to Bishop Walsh as a Clare selector so when he went down to Cork a month later he headed straight to Dr Con Murphy and asked, 'Up front now what happened with Jim Cashman and why didn't you change him?' Dr Con replied, 'Well we all agreed that Jim was being beaten and we'd have to change him. The problem was that none of the selectors could agree on who we would replace him with. So we decided to do the usual thing and give him five minutes in the second half.'

REST IN PEACE

When it comes to hurling Bishop Walsh has been known to breach conventional liturgical practice. He particularly recalls the funeral of JP Ryan. He was a selector on the Limerick hurling team from 1957 to the mid-eighties and when he was no longer a selector on the hurling team he became a selector on the Limerick football team. Hurling was his life. JP's funeral was extraordinary. Hurling people all over the country came. Sliotars and hurleys were used in the offertory procession, 'Faith of Our Fathers' was sung and there were addresses from the secretary of the local club, by the chairman of the East Board, by the chairman of the County Board and the Hurler's Prayer was said for the communion reflection. The theological purists were aghast.

Bishop Walsh was not involved though in another distinguished hurler's funeral that has gone into folklore. It was an awesome, if chaotic, sight. The spectacle of a bishop and a multitude of priests, crammed together like bees in a hive behind the altar, made a lasting impression on the faithful. Never have so many stood in so little space for so long. One of the priests had forgotten his vestments. As he was only five-foot-one, an old, frilly white alb was found for him. He looked like a cross between an altar boy and Tom Thumb.

The first problem was caused by the microphone. It seemed to have taken on a life of its own and emitted various crackling sounds at the most solemn moments. Such was the disturbance that some priest turned it off. This brought hazards of its own. The celebrants had to rely on vocal projection. While this was fine for the bishop it was less so for a Monsignor who always spoke as if he was suffering from a bout of tonsillitis. Those priests whose vocal ranges were somewhere in between seemed to think that they were obliged to break the sound barrier by shouting, rather than reciting, their modest contribution to the liturgical celebration.

The second problem was that everybody assumed that somebody else was organising the ceremony, so that nobody knew who was doing what or what was supposed to be happening. A priest would stand up to intone some prayer and just as abruptly sit down on discovering that at least one other colleague had beaten him to it. There were protracted pauses as everybody looked to the bishop to see what would happen.

Of course there was the choir. For reasons best known to himself the parish priest had taken a particular aversion to the choir, with the result that they were normally only to be heard at Midnight Mass and Christmas Day Mass. In the light of the musical talent which was evident on those occasions, his decision to employ their services so sparingly looked more and more judicious. Neither the organ nor the organist were in the first flush of youth, nor even in the second. The combination of two idiosyncratic performances made for interesting – if not elegant – listening. The choir predictably lived down to expectations. Even by their own standards they were abysmal. The problem was exacerbated by the fact that the assembled clergy seemed to have formed a rival choral group, apparently singing the same hymns at a different speed, to a different arrangement and musical notation.

The last straw was the prayers of the faithful, which the resident curate had arranged beforehand. The County Chairman had been asked to say one of the prayers as a recognition of the deceased's loyal service to the GAA. In a trembling voice he mumbled something indistinguishable, even to those in the front row. He gained confidence though with each word only to make an embarrassing faux pas just when his voice was clearly audible by praying for the hurler's immorality rather than immortality.

WHAT REALLY MATTERS

Willie Walsh has gotten to know many great characters through his love of hurling, particularly a character in Ennis called Paddy Duggan, 'the Duggie'. As a Clare minor Ger Loughnane's first introduction to inter-county hurling was under 'the Duggie'. Duggan gave a most amazing speech in the dressing room in Limerick. While whacking a hurley off a table and as his false teeth did three laps of his mouth he called on the team to kill and maim the opposition before saying an 'Our Father' and three 'Hail Marys'.

Duggie's whole life was hurling. When he became ill Bishop Walsh went to see him in hospital and Duggan had got the news that day that he only had a short time to live. He said to the bishop, 'I'd like you to do the funeral Mass and make all the arrangements.' The bishop agreed. Then the Duggie said, 'That's fine Willie. I still believe that we'd have won the county final last year if they'd listened to me at half-time.' As soon as the funeral was arranged he was straight back to the most important thing in life – hurling!

EDITED INFORMATION

The Duggie was not above misrepresenting Willie Walsh in his days when he was a humble priest. Both were mentors for a juvenile team in Ennis and in a club match Willie was stunned when all of a sudden he saw a young lad, Thomas Fogarty, being introduced as a sub on their team. He ran up the sideline to ask the secretary who had given the order to bring him on and he answered, 'Was it not you? The Duggie came up to me and said, "Fr Willie wants him in"!'

Three in One

The 2013 hurling championship was widely considered to be the best ever. In the All-Ireland semi-final Limerick faced neighbours Clare and brought a massive crowd. When Ger Canning told Clare mentor Louis Mulqueen about the huge number of Limerick fans Mulqueen calmly replied: 'A huge crowd to go home disappointed, Ger.'

That Christmas RTÉ marked the year with a special programme on the season. It featured a group interview with Ger Loughnane, Davy Fitzgerald and Anthony Daly. Ger Canning introduced it in a theological way: 'Ger, I guess you are God the Father. You [Davy] are obviously now God the Son. I suppose that makes you [Dalo] the Holy Ghost.'

It's Nice to be Nice

The effect of Clare's All-Ireland win was so overwhelming that Ger Loughnane did the unthinkable and wished Tipperary well. In 1997 he was quoted as saying: 'If Tipperary played China in the All-Ireland final we would be shouting for China.'

The Sound of Silence

The spat of the year in 2013 was between Ger Loughnane and John Mullane. That January Mullane announced his retirement from the Waterford team. After Waterford lost to Kilkenny Loughnane appeared to blame Mullane for retiring and for 'letting his county down'. Asked on Newstalk's *Off the Ball* about Loughnane's remarks Mullane appeared to be the bigger man when he replied: 'He's entitled to his own opinion. But I'm not going to comment on that.' However, he couldn't resist saying: 'I think if you're dealing with ignorant people, the only way you can deal with it is to ignore it.'

Up His Own Ass

The film *Four Weddings and a Funeral* made Hugh Grant a star. It also spawned one of the biggest selling songs of all time, Wet, Wet, Wet's 'Love is All Around'. On Valentine's Day in 2014 love was all around again – well almost. It was the day Ger Loughhane chose to write in his column in *The Star* that Offaly were the 'only team in the modern era with fat legs, bellies and ars*s'.

Twitter went into meltdown. Daithí Regan had a response that raised an intriguing biological question: 'Someone give Ger a replica Liam McCarthy Cup, stamp it 1998 "winners" then he might crawl back up his ass.'

CHAPTER SIX

GAA Management Made Simple

In 1884 Michael Davitt wrote: 'Old men who have forgotten the miseries of the Famine had their youth renewed by the sight and sounds that were evoked by the thrilling music of the camán, the well-directed stroke of the *cul baire,* or the swift stride of the gaelic forward in the pursuit of victory. Many dark days have dawned over our country. Sorrow and trouble have likewise made their way into the homes and hamlets of our people. It is certain that in some cases these clouds would have been darker and care would have eaten more deeply into the hearts of many had it not been for the pastime and pleasure [that came with] the revival of gaelic games by the Gaelic Athletic Association.'

The GAA has had and continues to have a massive cultural impact in Ireland. Gaelic games, especially when they involve managing a county team, are a very interesting and curious sociological phenomenon with their own specialised vocabulary. Many fans do not fully appreciate the nuances of these words. The following glossary of terms may help readers understand them better:

Meticulous attention to detail: *A nit-picker.*

Has leadership qualities: *Is tall or has a loud voice.*

Exceptionally good judgment: *Lucky.*

Strong principles: *Stubborn.*

Career-minded: *Back stabber.*

Relaxed attitude: *Sleeps on the job.*

Plans for advancement: *Buys drinks for all the lads at happy hour.*

Takes pride in work: *Conceited.*

Forceful: *Argumentative.*

Aggressive: *Obnoxious.*

Uses logic on difficult jobs: *Gets someone else to do it.*

A keen analyst: *Thoroughly confused and confusing.*

Of great value to the Association: *Gets to training on time.*

Experienced problem-solver: *Screws up often.*

The GAA is his first priority: *He's too ugly to get a date.*

Forward-thinker: *Procrastinator.*

Independent worker: *Nobody knows what he does all day.*

Good communication skills: *Spends a lot of time on the phone.*

Must be deadline-orientated: *We're already way behind schedule.*

Duties will vary: *Anyone can boss you around.*

A complex personality: *A complete nutcase.*

Some overtime required: *Some time each night and every weekend.*

Seeking candidates with a wide variety of experience: *You'll need it to replace the three guys who've just left in a huff.*

Problem-solving skills a must: *You're walking into a team in perpetual chaos.*

Requires team leadership skills: *You will have the responsibilities of management, without their pay or respect.*

Loyal: *Can't get a job anywhere else.*

Average abilities: *Not too bright.*

Exceptionally well qualified: *Made no major blunders – yet!*

Active socially: *Drinks a lot.*

Family is active socially: *Spouse drinks too.*

Character above reproach: *Still one step ahead of the Gardaí.*

Zealous attitude: *Opinionated.*

Quick-thinking: *Offers plausible excuses for mistakes.*

Careful thinker: *Won't make a decision.*

Keen sense of humour: *Knows a lot of dirty jokes.*

Expresses themselves well: *Speaks English good.*

Conscientious: *Scared.*

Fair: *Says that referees are only human, he thinks.*

Independent: *Needs no assistance because is perfectly capable of messing up on his own.*

Casual Work Atmosphere: *We don't pay you enough to expect that you will dress up.*

Apply in person: *If you're too old or too ugly or too whatever, you will be told the position has been filled.*

CRACKING THE CODE

Of course managers resort to a particularly sophisticated code to describe players. Below is just a representative sample:

He is a unique talent: *Sure he couldn't kick snow off a rope.*

He always makes the ball do the work: *He is lazy.*

He could get more out of the ball: *He is stupid.*

He has to train a little bit harder: *He is completely unfit.*

In fairness he has a powerful shot: *He never hits the target.*

He was a great minor: *He has not played a good game since he was sixteen.*

He is a good grafter: *He is a carthorse, a player with no skill, to be brought on as a sub at corner-forward, usually when the team was four goals down and playing against the wind and has not a chance of winning.*

CHAPTER SEVEN

Managerspeak

The former England rugby coach Jack Rowell was once asked what it was like to be a top rugby coach. He replied, 'You have fifteen players in a team. Seven hate your guts and the other eight are making up their minds.'

Managers say the most unusual things. Gary Lineker tells the story of his playing days with Leicester. They were playing at Birmingham and as they left the field a spectator spat on one of their players, who, unfortunately, spat back. The Leicester manager Gordon Milne gathered them around and said: 'This sort of behaviour is totally unacceptable. The next time someone spits at you, then you will just have to swallow it.'

GAA Managers bring great joy to fans – some when they arrive to a club or county but more often when they leave. Some are reputed to be paid a small fortune – but of course that can't be true because of the amateur ethos of the organisation. When it comes to contract negotiations you are not what you are worth, but what you negotiate. This chapter celebrates the many managers who prove the famous adage: 'It's a funny old game.'

MEDICAL MATTERS

A medical professor in Trinity College had just finished a lecture on the subject of mental health and started to give an oral quiz to the first years. Speaking specifically about manic depression, the senior doctor asked, 'How would you diagnose a patient who walks back and forth screaming at the top of his lungs one minute, then sits in a chair weeping uncontrollably the next?'

A bright young female student answered: 'A GAA manager.'

LOVE IS ALL AROUND

Former Cavan manager Val Andrews was meant to be christened Joseph but because he was born on 13 February, a midwife fuelled on love suggested Valentine when he was a day old.

Val's coaching career began at a young age. His earlier forays with underage teams were not always an unqualified success. After one of his half-time talks he looked out onto the pitch and instead of having fifteen, there were only eleven. In his own words: 'Four of them had f**ked off home.'

Val is a regular on radio programmes because he is not a man for soft talk: 'I don't agree with this Yankee school of "let's hug, kiss and breastfeed". Grow a set of a balls and mark your man that's all a player needs to do.'

BORN TO RUN

Managers have brought a number of new trends with them. Fitness gurus are all the rage. When the Iron Man from Rhode Paddy McCormack was training Offaly for a year his style of training was laps, laps and more laps. Eventually the players said to him, 'We're sick to death of all those laps. Tonight we're going to have something different.' Paddy thought for a moment and said: 'Okay lads that's fine. Turn around the other way for a change.'

MIXED BAG

There are no limits to the unusual situations managers find themselves confronted with as the following selection of heartfelt observations reveal:

Anxious corner-forward before club match in Sligo: Do you think I need gloves?
Mentor: For all the ball you'll get, it's not going to matter.

I warned the boys they couldn't go through the League unbeaten, and, unfortunately, they appear to have listened to me!
Tyrone Art McRory after his side's defeat by Donegal.

Kieran Donaghys don't grow on trees.

Liam Kearns.

Derry mentor: Seamus you're coming off.
Seamus: But we have only the bare fifteen.
Mentor: For the sake of the team you're coming off anyway.

The most important skill for any manager these days is to have a good excuse.

Tommy Lyons.

I didn't know what was going on at the start in the swirling wind. The flags were all going in different directions and I thought they must have starched them to fool us.

Mick O'Dwyer.

Fr Mick at the club's AGM: It's not the winning but the taking part that counts.
Club Manager Seán 'the straight talker' Smith: Father, that's the kind of sh*t* talk that sickens my hole.

WHAT'S SELDOM IS WONDERFUL

In 1982 when Seán Boylan took a call from Meath County Secretary Liam Creavin he was shocked to hear he was being offered the job as Meath manager. His surprise was greatly magnified though when it emerged that he was being offered the job as football manager. Boylan had played hurling for Meath for twenty years. When asked how rare it was for Meath to win in those games Boylan laughs: 'Rare. They were scarce as hen's teeth.'

LONG-TERM PLANNING

Boylan made something of a mark when he led Meath to the O'Byrne Cup in 1983. However, he really announced that Meath were a coming side when they won the Centenary Cup in 1984, the GAA's one-off competition to mark its centenary year. Boylan's wit was evident in the aftermath: 'Hopefully we can make a successful defence of it in one hundred years time.'

BOILING BOYLAN

For an entire generation, memories of Meath–Dublin clashes are linked inextricably to Seán Boylan. Graeme Souness said, 'I have come to the conclusion that nice men do not make good managers.' Seán Boylan is the exception that proves the rule: a lovely man, yet he has an inner steel to him. In 1987 he sensationally resigned as Meath manager because he felt that the team needed to make a bigger effort in training. The players asked Joe Cassells to ring him and persuade him to return. The call was made and a change of heart ensued. At the first training session afterwards Boylan said, 'I believe I owe you ten pence for the phone call.'

To riotous laughter from the Meath squad Cassells replied, 'Nah, it's okay, I reversed the charges.'

Tactical Confusion

Boylan has always been willing to let players know that their best days are behind them and carry out radical surgery on a successful team. A former Meath player of some note was speaking to Boylan about tactics after giving a less than distinguished performance in a challenge match. The player shrugged his shoulders and said, 'I'm confused, I don't know whether I'm coming or going.'

Boylan put his arm on his shoulder, looked him straight in the eye and whispered softly: 'I'm afraid, X, you're going.'

Aromatherapy

By profession Boylan is a herbalist. In 1991 after Meath finally beat Dublin in the epic tussle which needed four games to decide the outcome Seán was walking off the pitch when some Dublin fans poked fun at his vocation by saying, 'Get away ya bleedin' witchdoctor.'

Fear Crua

One of Boylan's protégés Colm Coyle took Seán's place on the Meath sideline – or at least he would have had he not been suspended. As a teak-tough defender Coyle embodied the stereotype of tough, hard Meath players and as a result had the odd problem with referees! I enjoyed Colm's reaction after the Monaghan team he managed some years ago beat Armagh: 'We planned for every eventuality, including if we had a man sent off. I told them what Meath did every time I was sent off!'

TALKBACK

Managers down through the years have produced more than the odd bon mot. Here is my top three:

1. We had to work very hard for this – it took 119 years for us to get it.

    Tyrone boss Mickey Harte after winning the 2003 All-Ireland.

2. Did you ever hear 'One day at a time, Sweet Jesus'? Before yesterday there were no All-Irelands in Tyrone, now there's one.

    Mickey Harte when asked about the possibility of two-in-a-row.

3. Every year we had a different trainer. In fact we had more trainers than Sheik Mohammed!

    Kildare's Pat Mangan.

ONCE AND TWICE

One of Longford's most celebrated sons is Eugene McGee who famously managed Offaly to the All-Ireland title in 1982. Although not the most distinguished player of all time McGee has a unique distinction as a player. He was sent off twice in the one game. He was playing in a club match for UCD and in the first half a player on his side was sent off but gave Eugene's name. In the second half Eugene was sent off himself but was too honest to give anyone else's name – so when the referee checked his report after the match he could not understand how he sent Eugene off twice.

O LORD IT'S HARD TO BE HUMBLE

As a manager, McGee first came to prominence in club management in the seventies with UCD. Legendary Roscommon footballer Tony McManus had some of his happiest memories in the game during his time in UCD between 1976 and 1980 under McGee's stewardship:

In 1979 I was captain and Colm O'Rourke was vice-captain. We became good friends. He was tremendously witty and sarcastic. Eugene McGee produced a newsletter about the fortunes of the team and he named the player who never shut up as the mouth of the team but he added that Colm was a strong contender! O'Rourke is very confident. The only time I ever saw him nervous was when I met him before the All-Ireland semi-final in 2007 when his son Shane was playing. He was never nervous when he played himself but he was that day.

From our Fresher's year Eugene had taken Colm and myself under his wing. He was a complex character but it was very enjoyable working with him. He certainly had a way with him. He commanded respect and had great ideas and was able to communicate them. There were lots of county players around at that time but he had no qualms about dropping them. Reputations meant nothing to him. You never knew what to expect from him. Days you thought you played well he might lacerate you. Days you thought you didn't pay well he would encourage you and compliment you.

My lasting memory of him came the day we had to play Queens. The night before was the Veterinary Ball and I had gone. The next morning he heard about it and was not happy. He made me travel with him in his car and never said a word to me all the way up to Belfast. In the circumstances I was really keen to do well and I scored 2–3. He said nothing to me after the match. Eventually when all the lads were gone and I was behind waiting for him in the dressing room to make the journey home he turned to the caretaker and said in his typically gruff accent: 'Would you have a jackhammer to widen the door a bit more? This fella's head is so big he won't be able to get out through it.'

DRINK UP

McGee has also spoken about the problems managers can have with a drink culture in a team. A new manager is dismayed with the drink culture in the squad taking over. He comes up with a brainwave to illustrate the error of their ways. He summoned the team into the dressing room and placed two glasses on the bench. One he filled with water, the other one he filled with vodka. He then dropped a worm into each glass. In the glass of water the worm lived, but in the glass of vodka the worm died. Afterwards the manager asked: 'Now lads what can we learn from this?'

One player snapped up his hand immediately and said: 'Drink plenty. It will kill all your worms.'

THE WHEELS CAME OFF

One of the biggest problems facing a manager is to get his players to train. McGee, before he resigned as Offaly manager, once threatened his squad that he would write a book of Offaly excuses. One Saturday afternoon in December, a player with a penchant for such excuses, turned up for training just as all the other players were walking off the pitch as he was wont to do. Eugene asked, 'Well what happened?'

'Oh, the wheel fell off my mobile home,' replied the player.

Just as he was about to make a sarcastic response the manager reflected that he had passed out a mobile home on the way to training and that the man's story could well be true.

JOHNO

Unlike Heinz, football managers come in more than fifty-seven varieties. It was said of one former inter-county manager in Connacht, 'The great thing about him is that his indecision is final.' That is never a comment that will be made about John O'Mahony. On Sunday, 24 July 1994 Leitrim's luck finally turned when they ended sixty-seven years in the wilderness to beat Mayo in the Connacht final by 0–12 to 2–4. Some people credited the win to John but others argued divine intervention was responsible. On the morning of the match a priest in Leitrim was said to have put a sign up in his church which said, 'Leitrim for Croke Park. Mayo for Croagh Patrick.'

UP DOWN

Down manager James McCartan Jnr steered his county to an All-Ireland final appearance against Cork. His talent was evident at an early age. He scored three goals in a McCrory Cup final and took Down to an All-Ireland minor title with his exciting and swashbuckling quality his bravery, his courage and his electrifying confidence and self-assurance. As a player he won senior All-Irelands in 1991 and 1994. His father had played on three All-Ireland winning teams in the 1960s and James had inherited the winning mentality from his dad.

I think the famous story told about him sums this up. When he was nineteen he played for Ireland against Australia in the Compromise Rules and was rooming with Jack O'Shea, one of the most iconic names in gaelic football. An Australian journalist asked him: 'What's it like to room with a legend?'

James shrugged his shoulders and said: 'You'd have to ask Jacko.'

WHELAN AND DEALING

2014 brought the normal toll of managerial casualties both in football and hurling. Despite the protestations of Joe Brolly, Gaelic games are now a results business. Many managers made the same assertion as Graeme Souness after he was sacked as Liverpool manager. Souness blamed his departure on the persistent hostility of much of the media towards him. As Ronnie Whelan, himself a casualty of Souness at Anfield when he was sold prematurely, incisively observed: 'Souness is complaining the papers had him sacked. They did. They printed his results.'

HELPS YOU WORK, REST AND PLAY

Thanks to Lance Armstrong, the issue of drugs and sport is never too far from the front pages. Colm O'Rourke had an interesting revelation about his Meath team when he joked: 'Seán Boylan had us drinking herbs that could also be used for stripping paint off the gate.'

GOING TO THE CHAPEL, GOING TO GET MARRIED

Jason Ryan's appointment as Kildare manager and the county's big victory over Louth in the Leinster Championship prompted one fan in Naas to resurrect a poster from 1998 saying: 'There's going to be a wedding: Sam Maguire is going to marry Lily White.'

CHAPTER EIGHT

Observe the Sons of Ulster Marching On

In recent years one of the ongoing controversies surrounding *The Sunday Game* pundits is the perception that the most high profile among their number have an anti-Ulster bias. One of their critics in this context is the acclaimed documentary-maker Peter Woods. The Monaghan native explains his passion for football in the following terms: 'Why I love gaelic football: all of life compressed into those seventy minutes, everything except death; well almost everything because Ulster is different.'

The main problem for the pundits is the way the top Ulster teams use their defences. After Tyrone triumphed over Kerry in the 2005 All-Ireland the pundits bemoaned the fact that Kerry were so badly served by the opposition they faced on the way to their final. Peter's solution to this problem was certainly original:

The logic of all this is overwhelming: for Kerry to compete against an Ulster team they must play in Ulster. Look on the upside, the Ulster Council's policy of appeasement of moving the Ulster final to Dublin has failed; we're still not liked down here. The Monaghan County Board want to redevelop Clones. With Kerry in Ulster there could be more games for the pundits to travel to north of Ardee. More rainy days in Clones, the chip wrappings fluttering about their ankles, traffic backed up on every road out of the town. Hell even AA Roadwatch would have to take notice. But the clincher is – just imagine what a boost Kerry would give to the Love Ulster campaign.

His view of the pundits is also unique:

So perhaps I shouldn't be surprised when football pundits cast Joe Kernan and Micky Harte as twin Voldemorts, bent on raiding the South and razing those citadels of fair play and champagne football in Kerry and Dublin: their only real opposition being those pundits, arraigned behind Pat Spillane, cast as Mad Eye Moody, and an uneasy Colm O'Rourke – given Meath's record – as Severus Snape, a foot in one camp and a toe in the genetic pool of the other. And there's Joe Brolly, one of our own, severely conflicted, glasses glinting like Harry Potter.

Isn't It Ironic

Pat Spillane is the best-known critic of Ulster football with comments like:

Right now playing positive attacking football is about as useful as trying to empty Kenmare Bay with a fork. There have been games this summer when if you wanted interesting viewing you would have been better off watching *The Angelus*.

The sad reality is that these cancers have spread throughout the country. Most tragically of all even my beloved Kerry have succumbed to this disease as was graphically illustrated in the Munster final. Regardless of how much natural ability a forward has there's not much they can do without the ball. As Con Houlihan once said of a struggling Kerry forward: 'He was like a gun-fighter roaming the streets without his gun.'

Spillane is not on his own when it comes to Ulster football. Kevin McStay had his tongue firmly in his cheek as he anticipated the throw-in of old rivals Tyrone versus Armagh: 'Welcome to the Pleasuredome.'

LATE TACKLE

They take football very seriously in Ulster, as revealed in former Ulster Chairman Michael Grennan's response to the suggestion that the IRFU would have the chance to use GAA grounds for their World Cup bid: 'We have prostituted ourselves and the bottom line is when you have prostituted yourself the people who make the money are not the prostitutes but the pimps. We'll know how much the GAA got for making Croke Park available but does anyone know how much the soccer or the rugby boys got out of it.'

The toughness of Monaghan football was emphasised in the old joke that a late tackle in Monaghan was one that came the day after a match! Ulster championship matches are renowned for their toughness. In 2002 former Monaghan manager Seán McCague in his role as president of the GAA expressed his unhappiness at the violence in the first International Rules test between Ireland and Australia. Reporting on McCague's disaffection on *Morning Ireland* Des Cahill observed, 'He said he wasn't going to support the serie's continuance.' Quick as a flash Cathal Mac Coille quipped, 'Do you think the Ulster championship is in danger?'

MARKING ANTHONY

Anthony Tohill was the star of the Derry team that won the All-Ireland in 1993. He always wanted to be a professional athlete. He is a huge physical specimen. As a teenager he had gone to Australia to try his luck at Aussie rules but came back when Derry started to motor. Team manager Eamon Coleman was keen to get him back. When he was twenty-four or twenty-five he went on trial to Manchester United. At one stage he was playing in a training match with the United squad. Although there was a hundred million pounds worth of talent on display Anthony was putting in plenty of sliding tackles and bashing into people.

Andrei Kanchelskis went to Alex Ferguson and said: 'Take that f**ker off before he kills someone.' Fergie went over to him and said: 'Son, I think we've just got to you a bit late in life.'

No Ordinary Joe

In the 1990s Derry football produced one of the great characters in the history of the game, Joe Brolly. In recent times though he has become something of the nation's sweetheart since he decided to donate his kidney to Shane Finnegan.

In 1993 Brolly was at the heart of Derry's most famous victory when they won their only All-Ireland. However, he jokes that because the county failed to win another All-Ireland he has become known as 'one-in-a-row Joe'.

The barrister has since gone on to become one of the most colourful analysts on RTÉ. Joe never really surrendered to managers and was never short of self-confidence. This did not always endear him to his managers. One of them was heard to say, 'He's down there now letting people know how good he is playing.'

The 1998 Ulster final between Derry and Donegal was, to put it at its kindest, something less than a classic. However, it produced one of the most dramatic finales ever when Brolly rounded Tony Blake in injury time to strike the decisive goal for Derry. He celebrated by blowing kisses to the terraces. That night the team returned to Henry Downey's bar and celebrated, in the words of Geoffrey McGonigle, 'until the birds were singing'.

Brolly's habit was to blow kisses to fans after he scored a goal. This caused one Derry fan to remark: 'At the best of times Joe Brolly is objectionable but when he blows kisses he's highly objectionable.'

Brolly wasn't always complimentary to his teammates. After a club game a disconsolate new recruit to the team said, 'I've never played so badly before.'

Brolly appeared surprised, 'You mean you've played before?'

After a county game one of his colleagues said proudly, 'That was the best game I ever played.'

Brolly said to him sympathetically: 'Never mind. You mightn't be as bad the next time.'

TRUE JUSTICE

Although he was a classy forward Brolly is most remembered for his flamboyant style. His exuberance did not endear him to his opponents: 'I remember once lobbing the Meath keeper in Celtic Park. He was a big, tall fella and I just popped it over his head. Colm Coyle came charging over to me and as I began my celebrations he drove his boot into me. I needed about thirteen stitches. Brian Mullins was managing us at the time and said: "You deserve, that you wee boll*x!"'

SELF-ANALYSIS

To his credit Brolly was also hard on himself. After a poor performance against Galway he said: 'My only consolation was that I held Tomás Mannion (the corner-back) scoreless.'

NOT A LION KING

Brolly also is honest enough to admit that he baulked at the prospect of playing International Rules for Ireland: 'I was asked about it a few times and I couldn't run away from it fast enough. I'm too much of a coward!'

A TALL TAIL

After Armagh beat Down in the 2008 Ulster semi-final the Armagh manager Peter McDonnell explained, using the term in its broadest sense, that: 'We were riding the donkey close to the tail.' An analyst is essential to the national TV audience in moments like this to decipher its hidden treasures. Happily Brolly rose to the plate and explained: 'Riding the donkey close to the tail? I presume that's something you do in South Armagh. It's a very odd part of the world.'

BROLLYISMS

Joe has left an indelible mark on the world of punditry. My top ten Brollyisms are:

1. He [Geoffrey McConigle] has an arse like two bags of cement.

2. I am as politically correct as a Nuremberg rally.

3. You don't like to put a dampener on the whole thing on the first day, because every team sallies forth with great hopes in their breasts but realistically only four or five teams can win the All-Ireland this year.

   Brolly's cheerful introduction to the 2007 championship.

4. He [Kieran McDonald] looks like a Swedish maid.

5. He [Conor Mortimer] would be better off spending more time practising his shooting and less in the hairdressers.

6. Why don't sharks attack Pat Spillane? Professional courtesy.

7. I was Derry's worst ever hurler. The manager used to shout at me: 'Kick the f**king thing.'

8. Cavan looked like ducks in thunder when they played Antrim.

9. Several of those players out there today aren't even the cousin of a county footballer.

Brolly on Cavan v. Down 2007.

10. *The final one requires some context: some sports stars like Katie Taylor are known for their modesty. Others are not. When Bubba Watson won the 2012 Masters David Letterman asked him: 'How would you describe your personal style of play, your personal approach to golf?'*
Bubba replied: 'Awesome.'

On The Sunday Game *Pat Spillane was in full flight:* 'I went on to Wikipedia to find out what I scored in championship football. I think I scored, I'm not too sure, thirteen goals and a hundred and fifty points. The point I'm trying to make, the bottom line … '
Joe Brolly: The bottom line, Pat, is that you're great.

BEAUTY AND THE BEAST

It is said that Brolly's favourite joke is: Quasimodo sits in his study and once again is feeling depressed about how ugly he is. Looking for some reassurance, he goes in search of Esmerelda. When he finds her he asks her once again if he really is the ugliest man alive.

Esmerelda sighs and she says, 'Look, why don't you go upstairs and ask the magic mirror who is the ugliest man alive? The mirror will answer your question once and for all.'

About five minutes later a very pleased looking Quasimodo bounced back the stairs and gave Esmerelda a great big hug. 'Well, it says I'm not!' Quasimodo beamed, 'Who on earth is Pat Spillane?'

RIGHT OF REPLY
So what then does Spillane say of Brolly?

Brolly is a top legal eagle. I told him about the lawyer who arrives at the gates of heaven. First thing the lawyer does is he asks to speak to God himself. He wants to know why He took him so early. 'Early?' God says. 'You're ninety-three years old!' The lawyer looks back at him and says, 'I'm not ninety-three. I am thirty-six.' Then God replies, 'Sorry, I calculated it in billable hours.'

While most people claim they never know what I'm going to say next I haven't a clue in the world what Brolly is going to say. He can be very infuriating. I would have prepared my contribution and planned to have a great joke ready and would be just about to use it when Brolly would butt in and say something nonsensical and burst out laughing and destroy my whole momentum. The opportunity to use my carefully crafted joke would be gone.

One of my few regrets about being an analyst goes back to 2003. The first round draw for the back door into the Leinster championship was being made. After the discussion on the glamour games we turned to a discussion on the so-called lesser lights. Brolly had long since lost interest and was getting very giddy. I was taking a great interest in what was going on and would always have a point to make about any match. On this occasion though Brolly's giddiness got to me and I got sucked into it as well. When we came to the last match, which involved Carlow, we were both giggling and seemed to be making a joke of it as if the match didn't matter. After the programme a lot of comments came in about how flippant we were and the way we degraded Carlow football.

At the end of every year I can normally stand over everything I say on television but this was one time I have to hold up my hands in the air and say Carlow football was treated with disrespect. It was that hoor Brolly that was responsible. He dragged me down to his level. It was wrong of me though to let him and I must acknowledge that.

Father and Son

In his role as an analyst on RTÉ Brolly defers to nobody, especially not to Colm O'Rourke or Pat Spillane. Away from the cameras the only man who Brolly defers to is his father, Francie. For his part Francie is always happy to put his son in his place: 'I played half-forward for Derry in the 1960s. Anyone who saw both of us play would agree that I was always a much better player than Joe ever was!'

Trinity Man

As an Irish schoolboy basketball international, Brolly did not follow the conventional path of Ulster footballers:

I didn't go through the St Pats Maghera, Jordanstown or Queens production line. My parents were folk singers so I boarded in St Pats Armagh and then I went to Trinity. One of my teammates in Trinity was Tadhg Jennings. He has a unique claim to fame. He is Kevin Heffernan's godson and in 1974 Dublin were struggling to find a free-taker. Tadhg was only eight at the time and he said to Kevin: 'I've seen a man up in Marino and he never misses a free.' Heffo was intrigued and went to see for himself. The rest is history. So many a time during my Trinity career I would hear Tadhg saying, whenever he had had a pint or two: 'I'm the man who discovered Jimmy Keaveney.'

WE NEED TO TALK ABOUT KEVIN

One of the many stories attributed to Brolly is of his experiences playing against Meath, and marking Kevin Foley in particular. A high ball came in between them, Brolly fielded it and in his own words 'danced around' Foley and blasted the ball over the bar. A second high ball came in between them with the exact same result. Brolly though was aware that the Meath crowd had gone very quiet and noticed Foley and Liam Harnan exchanging signals. The next ball that came in Brolly was aware of both Foley and Harnan coming at him at top speed so he ducked, causing Harnan to catch Foley with his elbow. Foley was stretchered off unconscious. Brolly claimed that he became a hero in Derry not because of any score he ever got but because he was the man who 'floored' Kevin Foley.

When questioned about the incident Brolly's characteristic smile appears: 'I am often asked since how hard I hit him. I just say: "Auch, I didn't go too hard on him."'

THE FIRST NOEL

Brolly is less reluctant to go hard verbally on a player. A case in point was his description of Cork's tough-tacking defender Noel O'Leary: 'He has the face of a man that is not always given to clean living.'

GIRL TALK

Brolly, though, was sometimes brought down to size:

Our manager Eamon Coleman was also crucial. He was jolly and a great character. He always played cards with the lads down the back of the bus. He was a teetotaller himself and didn't understand drink. Eamon was a small man so it was a sight to see him berating a giant like Brian McGilligan about drinking. The most enthusiastic drinker in the squad was Johnny McGurk. Eamon would say to him: 'Wee man, wee men can't drink.' The boys would be laughing because Johnny could drink any member of the squad under the table!

Eamon was a rogue but his heart was in the right place. He wasn't a great tactician but he was a real leader 'cos the boys loved him very dearly because he was a man's man. He once told me I needed to do weight training saying: 'Brolly you're like a girl.'

PAY FOR PLAY

Brolly is perhaps the most high-profile critic of the Gaelic Players Association. It can be exclusively revealed though that despite the amateur ethos the Derry squad were the first to engage in pay-for-play when they got an unexpected reward for their achievements.

Eamon brought us to Ballymaguigan one night and said: 'Lads there's someone who wants to speak to you.' In comes Phil Coulter. He was wearing a lemon suit and a lime tie. He presented each of us with a signed photo of himself and a commemorative copy of 'The Town I loved So Well'. The reason he gave us that was that when *The Sunday Game* came to film our celebration the night of the final we sang that song for them. On the cover of the record Phil had his arm outstretched in a Liberace pose. It was ghastly. It is gathering cobwebs somewhere in my house.

UPWARDLY MOBILE

Brolly got a new insight into sociological factors when he switched clubs:

> I gave up Dungiven when I was thirty-six because it was one hundred and thirty miles round trip and I transferred to St Brigid's in Belfast. I've got five kids so that eats into your time. It has given me a new lease of life. The club is based on the Malone Road. Bob McCartney, the controversial Unionist politician, made a great comment on the changing demographic about the Malone Road, which used to be home to the Protestant aristocracy but now belongs to the Catholic nouveau riche, he said, '*Tiocfaidh ár lá* has given way to *Tiocfaidh ár la-di-da*!' I became heavily involved in underage training in the club and you see all the Bentleys in the car park. We got promoted to the first division but I started playing in the fourth division. It was hairy enough there, particularly as you get punched in the back of the head as you are hearing: 'I'll give you a f**king All-Star.'

AGONY UNCLE

Brolly is also lighting up the world of social media with tweets like: 'If I have to endure marriage, I see no reason why it ought not be inflicted on the gay community.'

BACKCHAT

Actions have consequences. Brolly has also been the victim of some great one-liners:

Didn't you used to be Pat Spillane?

Confused Donegal fan.

The reason why I object to Ulster football is that it has inflicted Joe Brolly on us!

Pat Spillane.

You're no ordinary Joe.

Tommy Lyons.

What would finally help drag Brolly into the Premier League of GAA analysts is a copy of the *How to be as good an analyst as Colm O'Rourke* self-help book but it hasn't been written yet.

Meath fan.

Joe Brolly is proof of the tendency of stupid ideas to seem smarter when they come at you rapidly.

Fermanagh fan.

Brolly talks like Speedy Gonzalez on a caffeine high.

Armagh fan.

If they wrote a book about the nice things we say about Joe Brolly it would be shorter than the Amish phone directory.

Tyrone fan.

When two egotists like Brolly and Spillane meet, it's an I for an I.

Disgruntled Leitrim fan.

Brolly, you wouldn't get a kick in a stampede.

Tyrone fan.

PAYING THE PENALTY

In John McKnight's first year with Armagh seniors in 1953 they got to the All-Ireland final only to lose to Kerry. Armagh got a penalty and Billy McCorry took it. He was a great man to take a penalty and had never missed one before but, like Liam Sammon in 1974 – whose penalty, having never missed one for Galway, was saved by Paddy Cullen in the All-Ireland final – Billy missed.

Allegedly, Billy had been put off when taking that penalty because a Kerry player had run across him. McKnight was involved in an amusing postscript to the incident shortly after when he was playing for UCD in a club League game in Belfield. It went through his mind in that club match that he would do something similar to what that Kerry player had (allegedly) pulled off. After the ball was kicked he struck his foot out and the ball made contact with it and looped up high in the air and landed gently into the goalie's arms. The penalty didn't have to be retaken but there was a serious rumpus.

History repeated itself in 1977 when Paddy Moriarty had a penalty saved in the All-Ireland final by Paddy Cullen. Moriarty was forcibly reminded of the link between the two penalties in the graveyard at Bill McCorry's funeral when he was asked, 'How does it feel to be the only Armagh man alive to have missed a penalty in an All-Ireland final?'

KEEPING DOWN WITH THE JONES

In 1956 Tyrone narrowly lost the All-Ireland semi-final to the eventual champions Galway. The undisputed star of the Tyrone team at the time was Iggy Jones. The semi-final was a match that Jones was never allowed to forget. He had a goal chance to win the game when they were trailing by just two points. He made a run and cut in along the in-line. You don't score goals from there so he was looking for a teammate to pass to but there was no Tyrone forward there for him. The Galway goalie Jack Mangan was toward the near post. Jones thought to himself, 'I'll not get it past him but I'll get it over him.' He punched the ball over his head in the opposite direction to which he was travelling. Unfortunately Mangan got his hand to it and Tyrone's chance for victory was gone. Thirty years later Iggy went to a school to speak to the children and this boy came up to him and said, 'My Dad told me you were the man that lost the All-Ireland for Tyrone!'

CHAMPAGNE CHARLIE

Cavan's sole representative on the Centenary Team of greatest players never to have won an All-Ireland medal was the late Charlie Gallagher at right corner-forward. In 1964 Gallagher went to America for the Kennedy Games. On the trip he became close friends with Gerry O'Malley even though they were chalk and cheese in terms of personalities. O'Malley was very serious, religious and quiet: Charlie was devil-may-care. Every match Gerry played he had to win. Gallagher was always winding Gerry up and saying that if they ever met in a match he would destroy him – which drove O'Malley mad. In private Charlie admitted that he would have hated to have had to play O'Malley.

Down's Joe Lennon was on that trip too. He had written a book about gaelic football at the time and he brought loads of them out with him and sold them wherever he went. One day Charlie went up to O'Malley and said, 'You know what. I'm going to write my own book about football.'

'Really! And I suppose we're going to see Gallagher on the front cover in full flight with the ball?' asked O'Malley.

'You will in my barney. You'll see a big, juicy blonde!'

THE STRIFE OF BRIAN

One of the many incidents Derry's Brian Gilligan is remembered for goes back to one of his appearances for Ireland in the Compromise Rules series against Australia. The teams were coming off the pitch and one of the Aussies was chastising the Cavan midfielder, Stephen King. Brian was coming up behind Stephen and wasn't very impressed with what he saw. He went up and knocked the Aussie's gumshield out of his mouth and stamped on it with his foot. Nobody ever saw anybody shutting up so quickly.

WHO IS THE FAIREST OF THEM ALL?

Although he played with a very serious manner, Peter Canavan also had a light side. In 2003 he was speaking at a reception to launch his book. All the Tyrone team were there apart from the delayed Owen Mulligan. Canavan explained to the crowd that Mulligan was late because his mother had bought him a new mirror and he was still admiring his reflection.

LEG OVER

Canavan has showed a new side of himself since he has become a pundit with TV3. Commenting on the Munster semi-final replay in 2009 he remarked on the small dressing rooms in Páirc Uí Chaoimh: 'Senan [Connell] was telling me about a National League match that Dublin played here. It was so dark that one of the Dublin players, when he was changing, actually put his leg into someone else's shirt.'

FLYING WITHOUT WINGS

As a great player in the GAA, you have to be careful what you wish for.

Peter Canavan and Eoin Mulligan died and went to heaven. St Peter greeted them and said, 'I'm sorry, gentlemen, but your mansions aren't ready yet. Until they are, I can send you back to earth as whatever you want to be.'

'Great,' said Canavan, 'I want to be an eagle soaring above beautiful scenery.'

'No problem,' replied St Peter. And *poof!* Peter the Great was gone. 'And what do you want to be?' St Peter asked Mulligan.

'I'd like to be one cool stud!' was the reply.

'Easy,' replied St Peter, and Mulligan was gone.

After a few months, their mansions were finished, and St Peter sent an angel to fetch them back. You'll find them easily,' he says, 'One of them is soaring above the Grand Canyon, and the other one is on the bottom of a fridge in Omagh.'

THE LIFE OF RYAN

Tyrone's Ryan McMenamin was one of the most tenacious defenders in the modern game. In his own words: 'I know a lot of people think the way I act on the field is the way I act in life. If I did that, Jaysus I'd be in Maghaberry. I'd be in jail.'

This aggression was most graphically illustrated at a League game in Omagh in 2009 when he grabbed Kerry's fashion guru Paul Galvin in the groin area. Among a section of the Kerry GAA fellowship he was immediately rechristened 'Holden McGroin'.

MISTAKEN IDENTITY

In the early 1990s a certain club in Cavan was facing an intermediate relegation game. They fielded a ringer – a Meath county footballer, who a few years earlier had won an All-Ireland senior medal. He played under an assumed name. He caught the ball on his own forty, went on a solo run and scored a sensational point. One of the opposition management said: 'Jaysus, that lad is brilliant. He should be on the county team.' His opposing chairman muttered under his breath: 'He is.'

WHO SHOT MICHAEL COLLINS?

After Cavan lost to Tyrone in the Ulster championship a few years ago in a match they should have won the Cavan fans were dejected. Cavan's Cathal Collins had not had a good game and as he trooped wearily off the field the Cavan fans started shouting at him: 'They shot the wrong Collins.'

JACK THE LAD

Armagh finally reached the Promised Land in 2002 when they won their first Sam Maguire Cup. One of their great personalities was their goalie, Benny Tierney. In 2003 Benny went to San Diego with the All-Stars. As part of the trip some of the tourists went to see a NBA basketball match. Among the attendance was legendary actor Jack Nicholson. At one point in the game there was a controversial call and Jack was incensed. He rose to his feet and started screaming at the officials. When the torrent of abuse died down Benny rose to his feet and reprised one of Nicholson's most famous roles, in *A Few Good Men*, when he shouted, 'You want the truth? You can't handle the truth!'

COME DINE WITH ME

Armagh's pre-match breakfast menu provided Benny with another classic quote: 'It used to be a good old Ulster fry before matches, but we've changed that now to muesli – which tastes a wee bit like what you'd find at the bottom of a budgie's cage.'

NUDIE

One test of fame is when you are known simply by your first name: Bono, Gay, Seán Óg – no further introduction required. In gaelic football circles the name 'Nudie' elicits instant recognition as that of Monaghan's most famous footballer, Eugene 'Nudie'

Hughes. Nudie helped Monaghan to three Ulster senior football championships in 1979, 1985 and 1988.

Nudie was well able to hold his own in any company. One player who gave him a lot of problems though was the Kerry forward, John Egan. Ulster were playing a Railway Cup match against Munster and Nudie was marking John. They were standing talking because Nudie always talked to opponents even though he would be told not to. At one stage John said, 'What's that man writing down on that piece of paper? He's a right looking eejit isn't he?' As Nudie turned to answer John was sticking the ball into the net.

In 1988 Nudie used that same trick on Cavan's Damien O'Reilly. He was marking him in the Ulster final. At one stage in the game Nudie said, 'Jaysus there's an awful lot of people up on the Hill. How many people would you say are up there?' As Damien looked up to make his guess the ball came in between them and Nudie caught it without any obstruction and stuck it over the bar. O'Reilly was taken off him immediately.

Too Many Murphys

Nudie also made his mark on foreign shores. He played in England but his club game with Round Towers in New Eltham was cancelled. A few enterprising men came up from Bristol and got Nudie to play against Gloucester in a League final; totally illegally. He was the last brought on and about to hand his name, 'Brian Murphy' to the ref. The official from Bristol called him back and said, 'I'd better change that, as the other two I sent in were Brian Murphys and the ref would surely spot it.' They changed it to Aidan Dempsey and went on to win the match.

CLARE AND PRESENT DANGER

Monaghan were playing against Clare in a League match in Ennis. Some young lads started throwing stones at Monaghan's goalie, 'Bubbles' McNeill. True to form Bubbles started throwing stones back at them. The only problem was that he got so caught up with the stones that he completely forgot about the match. A Clare forward pumped a hopeful ball in from midfield and it went into the empty net. Monaghan lost the match by a point.

JIMMY'S WINNING MATCHES

Before Jim McGuinness there was something of a drinking culture among some of the Donegal squad. After the 2007 inter-provincial tournament that Ulster won in Croke Park, they were staying at Donegal legend Brian McEniff's Skylon Hotel in Drumcondra. Late in the night one of the Ulster squad asked where all the Donegal players were gone too. He was puzzled when he was told they were gone to the airport: 'Off to the airport. Why?'

'The bar at the airport doesn't close.'

THE JOY OF CESC

In the build-up to Donegal's 2013 All-Ireland quarter-final with Mayo while the tabloids were focusing on Cesc Fabregas' possible move to Manchester United Jim McGuinness spoke at length about his concern for his player's welfare in the light of the physicality of the tackles on them. Most pundits saw it as a thinly veiled attempt to influence referees. David Brady's verdict was: 'Jimmy's spinning matches.'

THE BOY FROM THE COUNTY ARMAGH

Kieran McGeeney captained Armagh to their only All-Ireland in 2002. As Kildare manager he has been involved in a few controversies. When questioned about them he had been known to exaggerate the situation: 'If anything goes wrong anywhere it seems to be my fault. Next thing I'll be blamed for the Famine and Fianna Fáil.' He has also been known to talk down some controversies, such as his sideline spat with the then Meath boss Seamus McEnaney, after which he said, 'It was more tickling bellies than anything else.'

The Fab Four

Of course what made Tyrone's 2003 All-Ireland victory all the sweeter was that it came over their old rivals Armagh.

Four men went climbing a mountain, each claiming to be the most loyal fan in the country: one was from Armagh, one from Tyrone, one from Tipperary, one from Waterford. When they climbed the mountain the Tipp fan said: 'This is how much I love Tipperary.' With that he jumped off the mountain and died instantly.

The Waterford fan said: 'This is how much I love Waterford.' With that he jumped off the mountain and died instantly.

The Tyrone man said: 'This is how much I love Tyrone.'

With that he pushed the Armagh man off the mountain.

Catch of the Day

Clashes between Armagh and Roscommon provided many memorable moments down the years. In 1982 they met for a series of three matches in America. Before the first match some of the players had partied too hard and went onto the pitch in something less than the full of their health. At one point the ball was coming in towards the Armagh goal. Their accomplished full-back Jim Kerr went for the ball but was experiencing a form of double vision and he went up for the ball but caught an imaginary ball, toe-tapped it and cleared it. Meanwhile a Roscommon player had caught the real ball and stuck it in the net. When interrogated about the mishap Kerr's response contained no admission of guilt, 'I got the ball I went for!'

FRANKLY SPEAKING

Tyrone legend Frank McGuigan was only the second player in history to play inter-county football at minor, under-21, junior, and senior levels in the one year. The first was Roscommon's Dermot Earley. Pat Lindsay played with McGuigan on an All-Stars trip:

> Frank was probably the most gifted player I ever saw though he would probably be the first to admit he was never a hundred per cent fit. He loved life! I roomed with Frank for a while. It was an education! One time we stayed out all night and in the morning we went to a diner for breakfast. We had a massive fry-up. A very nice waitress came over and asked if we had enjoyed our meal. Frank was a big man and he replied: 'It was so good I'll have the same again!'

POETRY IN MOTION

One of Ireland's greatest poets of the twentieth century Patrick Kavanagh was an abrasive character. He argued that all sporting subjects are 'superficial' as 'the emotion is a momentary puff of gas, not an experience'. The fact that Kavanagh's own sporting career was an unmitigated disaster may have fuelled his cynicism. Like Albert Camus, Pope John Paul II and Julio Iglesias he was a goalkeeper. In the early thirties he played for his local team, Inniskeen Grattans – succeeding Tom 'The Collier' Callan, who, in the words of his brother Peter, was, 'so stiff from farm work that he could only stop a ball that hit him'.

Kavanagh's most famous contribution was to wander off to buy either an ice cream or a drink, depending on whose version of events you listen to, while the opposition scored a goal between the deserted posts. The final ignominy came when he conceded the match-losing goal in the county final by letting the ball roll between his legs. His own supporters shouted, 'Go home and put an apron on you.'

His career as a sporting administrator fuelled even more venom. As club treasurer he kept club funds under his bed which prompted some nasty rumours. Like Father Ted who famously did not steal money but merely had it 'resting in his account', Kavanagh's own response to the innuendo was, 'It is possible that every so often I visited it for the price of a packet of cigarettes, but nothing serious.'

PREDICTION

Kavanagh once took time off work on the 'stony, grey soil of Monaghan' to attend the county final. He was asked to predict the outcome of the match. After a dramatic pause, he responded, 'The first half will be even. The second half will be even worse.'

HANDS UP

Kavanagh once let in two soft goals and one of the fans shouted at him: 'Use your hands to stop the ball.'

The poet replied: 'That's what the f**king net is for.'

DRINK, DRINK, DRINK

The Cavan county crest motto is: *Feardacht is Firinne*, which translates as 'Manliness and Truth'. One of the great exemplars of this was three-time All-Ireland winner Mick Higgins. Mick captained Cavan to an All-Ireland final victory in 1952 after a replay. The first match ended in a draw. It was the first time the GAA brought the two teams together for a meal after the game. When Mick and some of the Cavan boys got to the hotel they ordered drinks – just bottles of ale and a mineral. Mick went to pay for it but the barman said it was on the GAA. Mick double-checked if he had heard correctly. Quick as a flash once this was confirmed one of his colleagues said, 'Forget about the ales and get us brandies.' For the replay though there was no free drink!

GETTING HIS TEETH INTO IT

The New York born Higgins found that management was a more frustrating experience than playing. He often told the story of taking charge of Cavan for a championship match against Armagh. As the match reached its climax Cavan's dominance was threatened as Armagh took control over midfield. Corrective action was required urgently and Higgins decided to send on a sub, big Jim O'Donnell, whose high-fielding prowess was just what Cavan needed. Jim though didn't seem to realise the urgency of the situation. After going on to the pitch he strolled back to the sideline seeking a slip of paper with his name on it for the referee. Moments later O'Donnell was back again seeking a pair of gloves. Higgins forcefully told him to get back to his position immediately and not to mind about the gloves. A minute or two later he was back a third time to ask, 'Mick, would you ever mind my false teeth.' As he calmly handed the manager his molars Higgins blood pressure hit record levels.

PETER THE GREAT

Mick Higgins was the Ulster manager when arguably Fermanagh's best-known player, Peter McGinnity, played his first match for the province against the Combined Universities. There were two other Fermanagh players on the team with him, Kieran Campbell and Phil Sheridan, which was their highest representation ever as well as having Finn Sherry play for the Combined Universities. Four Fermanagh lads playing inter-provincial football on the one day was big news.

When the three Fermanagh lads went into the Ulster dressing room, first Mick said to Peter, 'Here you are Kieran, here's the number three jersey.' Then he turned to Kieran and said, 'Here's your number ten jersey.' It pulled them down a peg or two not to be recognised by Mick Higgins.

One of the funniest incidents in Peter's career happened in a club game when he was marking Barney O'Reilly. Barney enjoys the rare distinction of having won senior county medals in four different decades: in the 1960s, 1970s and 1980s with Teemore and a Meath medal in the early 1990s with Navan O'Mahonys. Barney and Peter played for Fermanagh under-21s together and they came up the ranks together. In one club match the ball went up between Peter and Barney's brother, also called Peter, and a kind of ruck developed. McGinnity snatched the ball as Barney came charging in to give his brother some 'assistance'. Happily for McGinnity in the melee and confusion Barney struck his own brother instead of his illustrious opponent. McGinnity headed up the field with the ball, before Barney started chasing him he said 'Sorry Peter' as his brother lay stretched out on the ground.

HAY EMERGENCY

One of McGinnity's teammates was the prince of midfielders, Derry's Jim McKeever. McKeever's happiest memories are of the club scene. His club, Ballymaguigan, were playing Coleraine in Coleraine. The pitch wasn't very well marked. The crossbar was only a rope and there weren't any nets. The ball was bobbing around and somebody pulled on it. One umpire gave it a goal, the other a point. Both umpires gave the decision against their own team. The referee split the difference and awarded two points. The really comic part of the story was that one of Ballymaguigan's best players, the late Michael Young, did not want to play as he had hay ready for baling and the weather forecast was not good. However, he was persuaded to play. When the controversy emerged Young went up to the referee and told him that he should hurry up and make a decision, as he had to go home to bale the hay!

Fleet of Food

McKeever played with Ballymaguigan in a seven-a-side match one evening. Before the match finished darkness was falling quickly. They had a famous character in the side at the time who they suddenly saw tearing up the sideline with the ball. They could not believe the speed he was going at. They found out afterwards the secret of this new found speed. As he was running he was not bothering to solo the ball but it was so dark that nobody could spot him.

Famous Seamus

In 1979 Monaghan qualified for the Ulster final against Donegal. The match is best remembered for an infamous incident. The referee threw in the ball. Donegal's Seamus Bonner won possession, sent in the ball to the forwards and one of the forwards popped it over the bar. The only problem was that the band was still on the far side of the pitch and they were playing the National Anthem! The referee had to restart the game and the Donegal point was disallowed.

Sudden Stop

Over his lengthy career Seamus Bonner was himself involved in some bizarre events. He was playing against Monaghan one day in a League match in Ballybofey and was soloing in with the ball twenty yards out from the goal with the defence beaten. He had goal on his mind but he had his mouth open and a fly flew in. He swallowed it and nearly choked. He was clean through and came to a sudden staggering stop with nobody near him and let the ball fall out of his hands and lost it. The Donegal fans did not know what happened. Bonner was not sure what they were thinking about but he's sure it wasn't complimentary. He believes that the moral of the story is when you're on a football field you should keep your mouth shut!

THE GLENS OF ANTRIM

The Donnelly clan, from beautiful Ballycastle, are the most famous dynasty in Antrim hurling. In 1907 Edward Donnelly co-founded the Ballycastle McQuillan club and was its first chairman. In 1989 his great-great grandson Dessie Donnelly won an All-Star at left full-back for his commanding performances which carried Antrim to the All-Ireland final that year.

Dessie has a special place in his heart for his teammates:

> In 1989 after we won the All-Ireland semi-final we were training hard coming up to the All-Ireland final. To get a bit of a break Paul McKillen and I went to see the All-Ireland football semi-final between Cork and Dublin. We were having a great chat before the game and as the players were coming on to the field I kind of noticed the big screen for the first time and I said to him, 'This should be a great game today.' Paul looked up at the big screen and then he turned around and asked me, 'Is this game live?' I nearly died laughing!

READ ALL ABOUT IT

A referee awarded a controversial goal in a club match in Armagh. The opposing players were infuriated and when he was jogging back to the middle of the pitch one of the players roared at him, 'That wasn't a f**king goal, ref!'

The referee responded, 'Check the papers tomorrow and see whether it was a goal or not.'

ONE MAN AND HIS DOG

Oisin McConville was playing and Pat McEnaney was refereeing. A dog ran onto the pitch and Oisin shouted at Pat to get the effing dog off the pitch …

Pat was hesitant as to how to handle the situation and Oisin said, 'Actually, better still, give the dog the whistle and you get off the pitch.'

CHAPTER NINE

Dub-le Trouble

In the 1970s Dublin brought new glamour to gaelic football. The Dublin players became like popstars and accordingly some of them had great appeal to women. One Saturday night one of the players took a young lady in his car up the Dublin mountains and got immersed in a passionate embrace. What they had forgotten was that the Don Tidey kidnap was on at the time and the Gardaí were on the look out for suspicious activities and suspicious 'vehicles'. The couple were at an advanced stage of undress and the car windows were very steamy when there was a knock on the window. The Dublin player had not time to react when a flash lamp was beaming on him. The garda was so embarrassed when he recognised the star of the Dubs that all he could say was, 'Can I see your driver's licence please?'

HUMBLE PIE

In the 1970s the great Dublin football team travelled down to Kilkenny for what they expected to be a meaningless feature against the county side. When they got to the ground they were very gratified to find a huge crowd in attendance to see what were spoken of as the greatest team of all time. The warm-up match was a club minor hurling championship fixture. When the mighty Heffo's army took the field their pride took a mighty dent. The ground was virtually empty because the majority of the crowd had gone home as soon as the hurling match was over.

LOST

Tommy Lyons was left eating humble pie when Westmeath shocked the Dubs team he managed in the 2004 Leinster championship. Everyone was gunning for him. He got an unexpected phone call later that evening from the world's leading filmmaker, Stephen Spielberg. Having heard about Ciarán Whelan's performance in the match he wanted to cast him in his next film, *The Invisible Man*.

After the game the story doing the rounds in Meath was that Lyons rang Mickey Harte after Tyrone winning the 2003 All-Ireland and asked what the recipe for winning an All-Ireland final was? Harte gave him the following drill: get loads of cones, place them carefully around the field, and have the players solo around them, doing one-twos, sidesteps, swerves, and kicking the ball over the bar.

After a few weeks Harte was surprised that Lyons had not rang him to thank him for his brilliant advice so he rang Lyons and asked him how they'd get on.

'Not great. The cones beat us by six points.'

DANGER

Many of the Dublin players did not play well on that day. One fan said of a Dubs player who really flopped on the day: 'The opposition are much more dangerous when he has the ball.'

A LOAD OF BALLS

After losing to Westmeath In 2004 the Dublin fans had to leave Croke Park behind for less salubrious venues, like Carrick-on-Shannon, for the qualifiers. The hard-pressed Leitrim County Board had a nasty surprise though when the Dublin fans took all their balls. We have had the 'Free the Birmingham Six campaign' and the 'Free the Guildford Four campaign' but after that incident Amnesty International immediately launched the 'Free the Leitrim balls campaign'.

PS I LOVE YOU

The Dubs' best known anorak is Bertie Ahern. As a Croke Park regular he is a keen champion of the sporting press. 'I love reading the sports pages. At least you know what's in them is true, unlike the rest of the papers.' Many of his utterances sound remarkably like a GAA manager: 'If hindsight were foresight, there wouldn't be a problem.' Some of his comments are as logical as a GAA pundit: 'I would never condemn wrongdoing.'

MEDICAL MATTERS

The late Mick Holden was one of the great personalities of gaelic football and hurling. Coming up to an All-Ireland final, Kevin Heffernan spoke to the Dublin team about diet and proper preparation. He told them if they had any problems sleeping before the final they should get tablets from Dr Pat O'Neill. The first person in the queue was Mick Holden. Heffo said to Mick: 'I never thought you'd have any problems sleeping.' Holden answered: 'Oh these are not for me. I sleep like a baby. These are for my mother. She can never sleep the night before a big match!'

BANK ROBBERY

One Saturday morning Holden was seriously late for training, much to Heffo's chagrin. The manager curtly demanded an explanation. Holden responded by saying, 'I was coming across town and I was stopped by the Gardaí. They said I was a match for one of the guys that pulled that big bank robbery yesterday.' A bemused Heffo asked, 'Really?' Mick answered, 'No, but it sounds so much better than saying I slept it out.'

Good Tactics
Former Dublin manager Pat Gilroy, noting the dwindling media numbers at one of Dublin's regular 8 a.m. press conferences, observed: 'I think we'll start at half-seven the next day and we'll be down to about four people. It is our best tactic of the year.'

Advertising
Bryan Cullen captained Gilroy's team to an All-Ireland in 2011. His acceptance speech was a little different from those of Joe Connolly and Anthony Daly because he included a plug for a nightclub: 'See you all in Coppers.'

Guinness is Good for You
In 1942 after Dublin beat Galway in the All-Ireland final a celebration took place the following November to mark the victory. It was during 'the Emergency' and rationing was the order of the day. Calamity struck at 11.30 p.m. when it was discovered there was no more drink. The County Chairman, a teetotaller, ordered for a further dozen stout to the tables. He dispatched one of the star players on the team, Beefy Kennedy, with a ticket for dozen stout. Weeks later the chairman was incandescent with rage when he received the bill. Beefy had switched the figure on the ticket from twelve to seventy-two!

Pay for Play

The GAA constantly speaks of its amateur ethos but it is not always honoured.

In 1946 Br MacCormack was the head brother in Crumlin CBS. He was shocked when his star player, a mere fourteen-year-old, walked into his office and told him that his mother had got him a job for fifteen shillings a week as a messenger boy. Br Mac Cormack told him that he would pay him a pound a week if he stayed in school because of his football powers.

The same player went on, to nobody's surprise, to become a star for Dublin. However, professionally he was not so successful but because of his profile was eventually offered a job on a building site. As he spent most of the time talking about his achievements on the football field he did not endear himself to his boss. Eventually his employer ran out of patience and he decided to sack him. He sent his secretary to tell the footballer that he wanted him in the office. The star player misunderstood the situation and thought he was being offered a promotion which he declined with a sigh; 'Ah sure, tell him I am not suited to working in an office.'

Holy Wit

The long relationship between the GAA and the Catholic Church is rich and complex. Although culturally and in many respects spiritually they were very close and the Catholic Church was to the forefront in promoting the GAA, the Church banned its priests and seminarians from actually playing inter-county football for years. Seminarians and priests had to assume a name to allow their footballing careers to continue at the highest level, despite the curious irony of men who so often preached the truth practising deception. Everybody knew who they were, including the bishop, but a blind eye was turned. It was a Jesuitical solution to a uniquely clerical problem.

Kerry is the only county that has produced a bishop who was the holder of an All-Ireland medal. In 1924 Kerry faced Dublin in the All-Ireland final. Kerry's Mundy Prenderville was a student priest in All Hallows College in Dublin at the time and was spirited the short journey down the road just in time to play and helped Kerry to win. Christianity is all about forgiveness but they took football seriously back then and Mundy was refused re-admission to the college after that! He had to find a new seminary to continue his studies and subsequently became Archbishop of Perth.

Although Mundy forgave All Hallows for their actions he did enjoy telling a story about a conversation he claimed happened in his time there. Following rigidly the rules whereby one must not complain about one's food, a young seminarian found a mouse in his soup, so he attracted the attention of the server, 'Please Brother! The student next to me has no mouse in his soup.'

Archbishop Prenderville saw the funny side of things. During Sunday service he explained, in the course of a long-winded sermon, why he had a plaster on his face, 'I was concentrating so much on my homily this morning while shaving, that I cut myself.' After the Mass as he was counting the money in the collection plate he discovered a note which read, 'In future, Father, concentrate on the shaving and cut the sermon!'

CLEARY, A PRESENT DANGER

In 1955 the late Michael Cleary was in line for a place on the Dublin team to play Kerry in the All-Ireland football final. The problem was that he was also attending the diocesan seminary in Clonliffe at the time. Under College regulations there was no way he would be freed to play the match. It was a straightforward choice: which was the more important to him: to play in the final or to become a priest? He chose to become a priest but as the final was being played he could practically see the ball down the road in the college. After his ordination he played for Dublin under the name of Mick Casey.

Years after his ordination he bumped into a well-known footballer who was clearly the worst for wear because of alcohol. He went up to reproach him, 'I'm sorry to see you are back on the drink. Haven't I told you before that the drink is your worst enemy?'

'Yes but remember Fr Mick the Church is always telling us to love our enemies.'

'That's true. But I can't ever remember them saying to swallow them.'

JAILHOUSE ROCK

Another time Fr Michael went to the local prison to visit a former club teammate who had fallen foul of the law. He asked the man what he was charged with.

'Doing my Christmas shopping early,' he answered.

'But that's no offence,' Fr Mick replied wide-eyed. 'How early were you doing this shopping exactly?'

'Before the shop opened,' admitted the convict.

While he was in the prison Fr Michael remembered the words from Matthew's Gospel, 'I was in prison and you visited me.' So he decided to visit some other inmates. One had such sad eyes and looked so lonely that he felt really sorry for him.

'Does your mother visit you often?' Fr Cleary asked.

'Never.'

'Your father?'

'Never.'

'Your brothers or sisters?'

'Never.'

'Why is that?'

'I killed them all,' the prisoner said with a whisper.

At that stage Fr Mick made a hasty retreat.

TO HONOUR AND TO CHERISH

Known as 'the singing priest' Fr Mick at one stage recorded an album. He also gained a reputation for his fast driving. Once his car broke down on the way to a wedding ceremony and he was an hour late on arrival. The wedding party was beginning to panic when he arrived, and he was so embarrassed he never forgot the incident. Twenty years later, he met the husband, a prominent former footballer, at a function and said, 'I'm so sorry about that horrible fright I gave you on your wedding day.'

'So am I,' said the GAA star. 'I've still got her!'

PICTURE THIS

Fr Cleary was a regular visitor to Croke Park. Once he was accompanied by a well-known but very cantankerous bishop. They were having their photograph taken by a press cameraman. The photographer had a lot of trouble trying to get the bishop to pose properly. Eventually, after much bickering, he was about to take the picture. 'Look pleasant for a moment,' said Fr Mick. 'Then you can be yourself again.'

One of his favourite stories was about the woman who went to confession. She asked, 'Father I was looking into a mirror and I decided I was beautiful. Was this is a terrible sin?'

The priest answered, 'Certainly not. It was just a terrible mistake.'

A CHRISTMAS TALE

Fr Mick claimed to have broken the world 100-metres record. The circumstances were rather bizarre. In the mid-sixties, when Galway reigned supreme, the singing priest was invited by a club in Galway to be their 'pretend Santa Claus' in a charity fundraising event in the local school. Fr Mick donned a white beard and red cloak in the normal way. He took his place beside a Christmas tree but was a bit puzzled to see that someone had decided to light a number of candles behind his chair. He started giving out presents and was really getting into the spirit of things when a young girl started screaming hysterically, 'Santa's dress is on fire!' Fr Mick looked down to see his cloak had brushed against one of the candles and was indeed on fire. The singing priest became the racing priest as he fled into the bathroom at great speed with a trail of smoke in his wake, a hall of children in hysterics and his dignity in shreds.

ASHES TO ASHES

Dermot Earley was a high-ranking army officer but for twenty years he was the undisputed star of Roscommon football. Traditionally the army had a mission every Lent. In 1979 the mission was given by Fr Michael Cleary. In one of his talks he spoke about determination and compared determination with Dermot Earley going through with the ball for the goal, much to the amusement of the rest of the congregation. On that Ash Wednesday Earley was going up to receive the ashes when Fr Cleary revised his blessing somewhat. Instead of 'Remember man thou art but dust and into dust thou shalt return' his blessing was 'Up the Dubs!'

MR DARCY

Declan Darcy should have been another Ross O'Carroll Kelly. Growing up in Sandymount in the heart of Dublin 4, an inhospitable, even barren, hinterland for the GAA, it was difficult to have foreseen in his childhood that he would become the face of Leitrim football's finest hour. The fact that both his parents were from Leitrim was the catalyst for his immersion into club football in the county, though initially the move was shrouded in controversy.

Darcy soon learned an important footballing lesson: 'I was marking Greg Blaney in a Railway Cup. I was just a nipper and because I respected him so much I was marking him very tightly and hanging on to him for dear life. Eventually he lifted me with an elbow and it was lights out. I couldn't see a thing. Greg is a dentist but he knocked out two or three of my back teeth!'

KENNY LIVE

John O'Mahony's Midas touch worked its unique magic in 1994. One of the iconic images of the year was Darcy, as captain of the Connacht champions, holding the Nestor Cup with Tom Gannon, who captained Leitrim to their only previous Connacht title in 1927. That was the start of an unforgettable adventure:

> I stayed in the Bush Hotel in Carrick the night after the game. The next morning the receptionist apologetically rang me and said she was being hounded by somebody who wanted to speak with me on the phone. I asked: 'Who is it?'
> 'Pat Kenny.'
> I thought somebody was winding me up but sure enough it was Pat who came on the line and asked: 'Where are you?'
> 'I'm in bed.'
> 'With who?'
> 'With the Nestor Cup.'

IT'S A KNOCKOUT

Although Leitrim were not to reach those dizzy heights again they did find themselves in the headlines once more:

> We were playing Mayo in a game live on RTÉ and a melee broke out and the Mayo manager, John Maughan, came running onto the pitch in his shorts. He passed a comment to Gerry Flanagan and Gerry floored him. In our view Maughan

150

definitely deserved it but its probably not the thing to do on live TV! Pat Spillane and the pundits were outraged but it did Flanagan's reputation no harm in Leitrim!

HOMEWARD BOUND

Some of the same fans who were throwing bouquets at Darcy in 1994 were swinging cleavers when he decided to transfer to Dublin, though many of his friends and Leitrim fans did wish him well:

We came very close in 2002 when Ray Cosgrave almost equalised against Armagh but to be honest I believe Tommy Carr had a better team. John Bailey, then the County Chairman, told us after the drawn game against Kerry in the All-Ireland quarter-final in 2001 that no matter what happened Tommy Carr would be staying for the next year. He actually cried with emotion as he said that but less than a month later he put the knife into Tommy. Players would have done anything for Tommy but we didn't do enough for him. I felt sorry for him because he was very unlucky, particularly with the Maurice Fitzgerald sideline that drew the match for Kerry the first day. Tommy was as honest as the day was long and was fiercely driven. There was nothing he wouldn't have done for Dublin. He was probably a better manager at the end but had more to learn and I think it's a shame he didn't get the chance.

I have never experienced anything like Thurles those two days. I had heard about Munster finals but was not prepared for the atmosphere in the square. It was amazing and packed with people. I remember hearing the sirens as the Kerry team were arriving and it was like the Germans were coming.

The Thurles experience did provide Darcy with the most amusing incident in his career:

> We were staying in the Horse and Jockey and I went out for a walk with one of the lads. A car pulled in beside us and my colleague said, 'There's your man.'
> 'Who?'
> 'Your man from *Star Trek*.'
> It was Colm Meaney and he was walking into the car park. The next thing I knew I heard a booming voice shouting: 'Hey Colm. Beam me up Scottie.' It was Vinny Murphy standing at the window. He was as naked as the day he was born!

FAB VINNY

Vinny Murphy was a larger-than-life character. He loved a fag. Somebody changed the sign in Parnell Park from: 'No Smoking' to 'No Smoking Vinny!'

JOHNNY BE GOOD

The 2013 All-Ireland football final did produce a great moment of sportsmanship. When the final whistle went you would have expected Johnny Cooper to have celebrated but he did not. His first instinct was to run over and console one of the Mayo players, Rob Hennelly, who is a friend of his from college. They won a Sigerson together with DCU. There was a picture taken of Johnny trying to console Rob and whoever said a picture tells a thousand words could have been thinking of this photo. It speaks volumes about Johnny and the way the game should be played.

Sadly, though, the Dubs' victory produced no quip to match Keith Barr after their 1995 All-Ireland: 'There won't be a cow milked in Finglas tonight.'

Private Session

Two days after the All-Ireland final it was decided that some of the Dublin players would have a private session. Footballer of the year Michael Darragh Macauley was one of the organisers. He took a call from a member of the team looking for directions to the secret venue. His friend was well 'refreshed' as he rang the doorbell of the given address in a state of high spirits. The blood drained from his face though when the door was answered by Jim Gavin's wife. Macauley had deliberately sent him to the manager's home in an effort to embarrass him. He succeeded. The player's one hope was that Mrs Gavin would not recognise him. She did.

CHAPTER TEN

Galway Boys Hurrah

No discussion on gaelic games would be complete without reference to 'the Master', Seán Purcell, who is often spoken of as the greatest player of all time. According to legend, following Galway's All-Ireland win in 1956 Seán Purcell was waiting one day for the bus from Galway to Tuam, not realising that the last bus had gone. A driver was on his way back to the garage with an empty bus when he spotted the Master and although it was against all regulations he stopped and asked him where he was going. When Purcell told him Tuam, the driver said 'Hop in'. Four miles out from Tuam the poor man nearly had a stroke when he saw an inspector standing in the middle of the road waving him down. The inspector was a seething mass of anger and demanded an explanation. 'I have the Master here,' answered the driver meekly.

'The Master. You can't be serious!' said the inspector, boarding the bus to verify the fact. When he saw the evidence with his own eyes he turned angrily to the driver again.

'How could you be so stupid? Turn around and get back to the garage straight away. How could you drive the Master in just a single-decker bus. Get him a double decker straight away so that he can go upstairs if he fancies a cigarette.'

BACKHANDED COMPLIMENT

With a twinkle in his eye the Master's son John recalls his father's mischievous nature:

> Daddy had a great capacity to become friends with a large section of people. Seán Óg Ó hAilpín was just one of the people who visited him in hospital. He became very friendly with the Dublin team of the 1970s through his role in managing the All-Stars, especially with Tony Hanahoe. They have a charity function every year and present Hall of Fame style awards. The night before Dad died they were presenting Martin O'Neill and himself with an award and I was accepting it on his behalf. I asked him had he any message for them. He replied: 'Tell them before I got to know them I thought they were a crowd of f**kers but once I got to know them I didn't think they were too bad!' I said a softer version of that on the night!

FAME IS FLEETING

John recalled when his Dad was cut down to size:

> One time he was collecting an award himself up north and the emcee was going on and on about how great a player Daddy had been. Daddy grabbed the microphone off him mid-flow and said: 'Don't think I'm that famous. I ran for election once. Both John Donnellan and I were running for Fine Gael for the one seat in 1965. I barely got my deposit back and was lucky to get even that and John was easily elected. As I was leaving the count centre, crestfallen, a woman called me over and said: "Don't worry Seánin, there'll be another day. Isn't it a pity you didn't play a bit of football!"'

THE COMEBACK KID

During the late 1970s the All-Star team were managed by Seán Purcell. Seán called out the team before the first game and announced that he was playing half-forward. That got a great laugh but Seán turned on them and said in all earnestness: 'What's so funny lads?'

JACK THE LAD

One of Purcell's teammates was Jack Mahon. Jack once bumped into a young fella in Galway and was a bit disappointed to hear that the youngster had never heard of him. He hoped he might impress his new acquaintance when he told him that he played at half-back on the Galway team that beat Cork in the 1956 All-Ireland final.

'Gosh that's shocking,' said the youngster.

'Why?' asked a bemused Jack.

'Because I've just discovered my Dad's a liar. He's always said that when Galway won that All-Ireland they never had a centre-back!'

NO JOHNNY-COME-LATELY

One of the stars of the Galway team in the 1970s was Johnny Hughes. Although he does not have the All-Ireland medal his great talent deserved he has many happy memories from his time with Galway and some hair-raising experiences.

When the Galway team were training in Tuam there would always be players looking for shampoo afterwards. Johnny always had shampoo but Thomas Tierney and Tommy Joe Gilmore were always swiping some off him. Johnny was working for a chemical company at the time who manufactured a light oil which looked like Clinic shampoo. He poured some of it into an empty bottle of shampoo, which he left outside his shower in the dressing room.

He hid a bottle of shampoo in his bag and he went in to the shower with some of it in his hand. A few seconds later he saw Tierney's foot coming over and taking the bottle of shampoo but Johnny didn't let on to see him. Tierney rubbed it into his hair and passed it on to Tommy Joe. A few minutes later all hell broke loose. The incident stopped them from stealing Johnny's shampoo for a long time after that.

UNWELCOME PRAISE

History has forged a peculiarly close bond between the five counties in Connacht. No other province has had to live with a noose as great as 'To hell or to Connacht' around its neck. Nonetheless the solidarity off the field is only matched by the intense rivalry between the counties on it. Johnny Hughes was to get a loud reminder of it in 1999. He went to the replay of the FBD League final in Tuam with Mattie McDonagh. There were two fans from Roscommon behind them and they knew who the two former Galway greats were and during the whole match they kept shouting into their ears about how wonderful Roscommon were. After the match was over and Galway were beaten Johnny turned around to Mattie and at last the two lads were silent for a minute because they wanted to hear what he said. His comment was, 'In all fairness to Roscommon they always were a great winter team.' The two Roscommon boys were absolutely disgusted.

CLERICAL ERROR

Hughes found a new outlet for his skills when his inter-county career finished through his involvement in charity matches with the Jimmy Magee All-Stars. Johnny always did a running commentary on those matches as he was playing in them, much to Jimmy's delight.

One day before a match Johnny heard Jimmy giving the team-talk to boost the team's morale. He put his hand on his wing-back Fr Brian Darcy's shoulder and said, 'Brian, in years to come GAA people will be sitting around their fires and they'll be talking about the great wing-backs of all time ...' As he paused and you could see Brian's chest swelling with pride, 'and you know something Brian, when they do – you won't even get a mention.'

TUNNEL VISION

Brian Talty has already chosen his epitaph: given that he experienced the fate so many times as a player, as a coach, and selector it is: 'We were beaten by a point.'

The disappointments in the Connacht championship in those years were offset by victories in the Gael Linn competition:

The prize for winning it was a trip to New York so that's why we put more into winning it than the Connacht championship! We had some great times on those trips. My abiding memory is of rooming once with Billy Joyce. We were staying in the Taft Hotel. It should've been called the Daft Hotel! One day Billy was lying on the bed when one of our teammates came rushing into the room in a state of high excitement shouting: 'I've just got the news that I've won an All-Star.'

Billy coolly looked up him and said: 'Didn't I tell you that you'd get one?'

Our colleague beamed and said: 'You did.' Then modesty took over and he added: 'I didn't deserve one.'

Billy's response was immediate: 'Correct.'

GILMORE'S GROIN

In 1983 Talty's Galway team showed all the signs of a good team when qualifying for the All-Ireland final: they won without playing well.

Living and working in Dublin, I was trying to keep away from the hype as much as possible, which wasn't easy. I was having a tough year. I had a stomach injury for most of the season and was spending a lot of time on the physio's table. Nowadays there would probably be a name for the condition like 'Gilmore's groin' (after the great Galway star TJ Gilmore) but back then there wasn't much understanding. My mother said: 'It's all in your head.'

Billy Joyce never believed in injuries and met me one day when I was going to see someone who had a good reputation for dealing with my condition. When I told him where I was going he said: 'For Jaysus' sake if I told you there was an auld wan with a magic cure you'd go to her.' Years later I met him in Tuam on crutches and asked him what had happened. He told me that he was getting out of his car and he tore his Achilles tendon. I told him it was all in his head!

LET'S BE FRANK

Talty's trips to America with the All-Stars did create some lasting friendships:

Frank McGuigan was a great tourist. He'd play games after having had a few pints and still go out and grab great balls out of the air. I always wondered what he'd be like if he had no pints!

TACTICAL INNOVATION

Talty saw some unorthodox tactical manoeuvres on those trips:

One of my clearest memories is of playing at centre-field in Gaelic Park against Kerry. They had come up with this revolutionary move at the time, everybody does it now, which involves the midfielders switching sides. Tom Spillane had just come on the scene and I remember looking at my midfield partner Moses Coffey and saying: 'What the f**k is happening?' The second match was in San Francisco and before it Moses came to me and said: 'Don't worry. I will sort things out today.' The first ball that came our way I heard a screech of pain and saw Tom Spillane sprawled out on the ground. There was no more crossing over that day!

HIGH FIELDING

Laughter regularly punctuates Talty's conversation. Perhaps that explains why he looks as if he is set to become the Peter Pan of gaelic football. The laughter is accentuated whenever Billy Joyce is brought into the conversation:

Once before we played a big match in Croke Park Billy took us by surprise by asking: 'Did ye ring the airport?' I didn't know what he was talking about and asked him why would we ring the airport. He replied: 'To tell them not to have aeroplanes flying over Croke Park. I'm going to be jumping so high I don't want to be in collision with them.'

THE HARDER THEY FALL

Billy Joyce was not a man to take prisoners:

When we were getting beaten in midfield by a particular player Billy would turn to me and say: 'Time to take the chopper out.' The next ball that came our way you would hear a thud and a sigh of pain.

We were playing Roscommon in Pearse Stadium and it was an atrocious wet day. Before the throw-in one of their midfielders said to Billy: ''Tis an awful day for football.' Billy looked at him and said: 'You don't have to worry about it. You won't be out in it very long.' He was right!

SALMON LEAP

In the early 1990s Connacht footballers were invariably free in August and September and many took the route of weekend tourist for transatlantic games.

Before their glory days of 1998 Galway were knocked out early in the championship one year and a famous man in the GAA in New York, Jackie Sammon, rang Val Daly and asked him to travel over to line out for Connemara Gaels the following Sunday and to bring a couple of other good players with him. Daly rang around and persuaded former Galway full-forward Brian O'Donnell to travel with him. Brian had never played in a match in New York. The two lads flew out on the Friday evening and on the plane Daly briefed his colleague on how to get through the weekend. He said, 'Now Brian they do things differently over there. It's not like at home so just enjoy the weekend, play the match and don't mind what anyone says. Whatever you do, say nothing.'

The Tribesmen enjoyed the first part of the weekend but the match went less well. At half-time the Connemara Gaels were seven points down. Jackie Sammon gave a team-talk and said, 'Ye're the most disgraceful shower I ever saw. Ye're a disgrace to the Connemara Gaels jersey. As for the big shots from over in Ireland I'm sorry I brought ye out at all. Daly you were hopeless and O'Donnell you were even worse. You didn't even catch one ball.'

O'Donnell forgot Daly's advice and retorted, 'Sure how could ye play football out there. There wasn't a single blade of grass on the pitch.'

Sammon turned around to him and asked, 'Did you come out here to play football or to graze?'

MULTITALENTED

John O'Mahony's All-Ireland winning team was full of talented players, with exceptional skills from the searing runs of Michael Donnellan to the famous sidestep of Ja Fallon. Willie Hegarty paid tribute to one of them: 'Padraic Joyce sold more dummies than Mothercare.'

In the wake of Galway under-21 victory over Cork in the All-Ireland final and Luis Suárez's bite on Branislav Ivanović in 2013 Willie wrote in the *Roscommon Herald*: 'The current Galway under-21 team has more bite than Luis Suárez.'

AT DEATH'S DOOR

A Gaeltacht club in Galway called Michael Breathnach's had a junior manager and he was trying to round up a team for a match. He rang one seventeen-year-old and asked: 'There is a match on Saturday, are you able to play with us?'

The young fella replied: 'No, I am going to Oxegen on Saturday.'

The manager had no idea that Oxegen was Ireland's premier music festival and thought the young lad was going to hospital for some respiratory problem. He said: 'I'm so sorry, look after yourself.'

He rang three or four young lads in the local area and they all told him they were off to Oxegen and he thought there was some epidemic around the local area.

Later that night, he was down in the pub giving out yards about the fella who gave him the phone numbers of the young lads and he said: 'Your man gave me number of lads on their deathbeds.'

THE MANAGERIAL MERRYGROUND

Johnny Giles once said: 'The team with the least "ifs", "buts" and "ands" always wins the championship.' There is a lesson for everyone there. Galway footballers have changed managers with alarming regularity in recent years.

After Joe Kernan retired as Galway manager he subsequently met his successor, Alan Mulholland. He wished Mulholland the best of luck and ushered him aside, 'Just a little advice, as tradition goes from one outgoing Galway manager to the next, take these.'

He handed him three envelopes.

'If you fail to lead Galway to victory,' he said, 'open an envelope, and inside you will find some invaluable advice as to how to proceed.'

Mulholland got off to a flyer and Galway had a crushing victory away to Roscommon in the Connacht championship in 2012. Then when Galway lost to Sligo things started to go badly wrong. Mulholland remembered Kernan's envelopes and after that bad defeat he opened the first envelope. 'Blame the referee,' it said.

He walked confidently into the informal press conference and said, 'Well, there wasn't much between the teams really. In a match like that small mistakes can change the complexion of the game completely and in that respect I felt that the ref made some decisions that went against us which had a big bearing on the final outcome.'

The journalists nodded wisely. Kernan's advice was working well.

Another embarrassing defeat to Antrim quickly followed in the qualifiers. Bad news, Mulholland would have to use the second of the three envelopes.

'Blame the free-taker,' it said. Off Mulholland went to face the media.

'Well. I thought it was nip and tuck, we had them under pressure. We tried a few different lads taking our frees, but unfortunately we didn't have the best of days with the old shooting boots and so the chances slipped away.'

Again the journalists seemed satisfied with his response. Thank God for these get-out-of-jail-free envelopes Mulholland reflected, though he still had failed to take Galway forward which he knew was storing up trouble for himself.

In 2013 after Galway crashed out of the championship to Mayo Mulholland was heartbroken and gutted by the scale of the humiliation. There was only one consolation, help was at hand. He walked into the dressing room, looking forward to some first-class advice from the third and last white envelope. He rummaged in his bag, pulled it out and tore it open. The advice was simple, 'Start writing out three new envelopes.'

When Revenge is not Sweet

One of the talking points of the 2013 championship was Eamonn O'Hara's severe criticism of his former Sligo manager Kevin Walsh on *The Sunday Game*. From his days playing for Galway Walsh has more amusing memories:

> We were away on a team holiday and Seán O'Domhnaill was messing and pulled down the togs of let's say a prominent County Board official in full view of everyone. Needless to say the man in question was not too happy. Later, when Seán was sunbathing on the beach the official sneaked up and took the wallet which was lying beside him. When he figured out what was happening Seán ran after him down the beach. They were not a physical match and Seán was catching up with him so your man threw the wallet into the ocean. He couldn't understand when Seán started laughing. The wallet belonged to Ja Fallon's wife and she asked Seán to mind it while she went for a swim!

THERE'S NO SHOW LIKE A JOE SHOW

The rich history of the GAA is studded with personalities who have retained forever a place in the memory of those who have had the good fortune to see them in action.

Joe Canning is unusual in that he had already gained a place in the hurling immortals when he was a teenager, given his exploits with his club Portumna and with Galway's underage teams, winning two minor All-Irelands and captaining the team as they sought a three-in-a-row, only to lose to Tipperary. Canning is a sportswriter's dream: boy-next-door manner, quick-witted, intelligent and above all immensely talented.

Canning's exploits have elevated him to the status of hero but his innate self-possession has saved him from being overwhelmed by the celebrity that has engulfed him. His self-depreciation is most evident in the tagline of his former Bebo page, which read: 'Slow and one-handed.'

A QUIET NIGHT IN

The most famous quote in the hurling vernacular is Micheál Ó Muircheartaigh's observation: 'A mighty poc from the hurl of Seán Óg Ó hAilpín … his father was from Fermanagh, his mother from Fiji, neither a hurling stronghold.'

However, a good contender for runner-up must be: 'Sylvie Linnane: the man who drives a JCB on a Monday and turns into one on a Sunday.'

Few hurlers generated the same drama on the pitch as Sylvie Linnane. However, it is a little-known fact that Sylvie once created a drama off the pitch:

We were in Dublin the night before an All-Ireland final and as always we were sent to bed early. The problem is that it is very hard to sleep the night before an All-Ireland. I was rooming with Steve Mahon and we heard a massive row going on in the street underneath. So I went to investigate and saw this fella beating up his wife or his girlfriend. I ran into the bathroom, got the waste-paper basket filled it with water and ran over to the window and threw the water over the man. It did the trick and he stopped and the woman ran away. A happy ending or so I thought until the man recovered from the shock and got really, really angry and started to climb up the drainpipe to pay back the person who threw the water on him. I didn't think the night before the All-Ireland was the best time to get involved in a brawl – especially as this guy looked like a pure psycho and I decided discretion was the better part of valour. I turned off the light so he wouldn't know where to find me. I went quietly back to bed and listened attentively to see what would happen. What I hadn't known at the time was that the light immediately below my room was on! The room belonged to the former Galway great Inky Flaherty. Inky was not a man to mess with and a few minutes later I heard him forcefully eject the intruder out the window – which was not the typical way to prepare for an All-Ireland.

NICE ONE CYRIL

Cyril Farrell once revealed an enterprising side to Linnane's character:

Sylvie loved a nice hurley. He always travelled to training with Seán Silke. Silke and Iggy Clarke used get the hurls for us. Silke would usually have hurls in his boot. When Sylvie needed a hurl he would get out of the car as Seán left him home after training to get his gear and sneak off with the hurl he liked most. The next day Seán would ask him if he took the hurl. Sylvie would always deny it point blank. Then a few weeks later he would casually stroll into training with the missing hurl!

GOING BRAVELY WHERE NO ONE HAS GONE BEFORE

Noel Lane was another of the stars on the Galway team. One of the funniest memories from Lane's time with Galway is of a trip abroad:

> We went to America on the All-Star trip and brought a big contingent of Galway supporters with us. We visited Disneyland and a gang of us went on the Space Mountain ride. I was sharing a carriage with Steve Mahon and some of the lads like Finbarr Gantley were behind us. Two of the most 'mature' members of the group, John Connolly's dad, Pat, and Mick Sylver were behind them. After we came down we were all petrified and just glad to have got out of there alive. We went to a little bar nearby to catch our breath back. Just as we started to relax who did we see in the queue to go back up Space Mountain but Pat and Mick!

PREACHER MAN

Having won four All-Star awards, Fr Iggy Clarke retired at the tender age of thirty-two in Centenary Year. In 1997 Clarke left the priesthood and is now married. However, it was his experiences in the priesthood that provided him with his most amusing memory from his career:

> The morning of the All-Ireland final in 1981 I was saying Mass for the team in the hotel. The gospel that day was about the parable of the mustard seed: the smallest grows into the biggest seed. In my sermon I gave a very eloquent philosophical presentation on how the story of the mustard seed equated with our journey as a team. In '75 we were a tiny seed but in '81 it would really go into fruition. That night at the meal we were all down because we felt we had left another All-Ireland behind us. Joe Connolly turned to me and said: 'Jaysus whatever happened to that f**kin' mustard seed!'

CHAPTER ELEVEN

Tipp Top

Hurling was once cynically described in a British Sunday newspaper as 'cavemen's lacrosse'. In the debate as to whether hurling or football is the greatest game on earth there is only one answer in Tipperary; hence Tony Wall's adage: 'Football is a game for those not good enough to play hurling!'

Tipperary have given the game great players and characters, though nobody could top Mick 'Rattler' Byrne. He was a small man but pound for pound he was the toughest man you could ever meet. He could mark guys from Wexford three or four stone heavier than him but he would never be beaten. He was a great corner-back for Tipp but also a wonderful storyteller. He did not have much time for all the talk players have today about their injuries, especially about their 'hamstrings'. He always said that the only time in his playing days he heard anybody talking about hamstrings was when they were hanging outside a butcher's shop.

Byrne went to New York with Tommy Doyle, who was making his first flight and was very nervous. He sought comfort from the Rattler who told him, 'Don't be worrying Tommy. There are two parachutes under the seat, you put one on, jump out, count to ten, press the button, and you jump to safety. What could be simpler?'

'But what happens if the parachute doesn't open?' asked Tommy.

'That's easy,' answered the Rattler, 'You just jump back up and get the spare one.'

THE MIGHTY QUINN

In the 1950s one of Tipperary's star forwards was a young Billy Quinn, whose three goals in the 1954 League final ensured that Tipp beat Kilkenny that day. Billy is the father of Niall, who served Irish soccer with such distinction. Although soccer claimed Niall's career his love of hurling remained unabated.

Niall's uncle Niall was also a fine hurler. Back in the 1940s one summer he was selected to play for Tipperary against old rivals Cork in a championship match – which was a dream come true for any hurler. Niall arranged to be picked up by teammates outside a pub called Horse and Jockey. As he waited for his lift he spotted a red squirrel. So taken was he by the squirrel that he decided he would pass up the opportunity to play against Cork so that he could catch the squirrel and make it his pet. Hours later he returned home in triumph with his prize to be greeted by baffled neighbours who wondered why he hadn't lined out for Tipp. Quinn had no regrets. He played again for Tipp and kept the squirrel for years.

DOING BABS KEATING

Despite his pride at his son Niall's great success in soccer, Billy Quinn still feels the game is no match for hurling. He put his foot in it in 1990 when a journalist came to interview him about Niall after he scored the famous goal against Holland in the World Cup. When he asked Billy if he was proud of Niall, Billy said without thinking, 'To tell you the truth I'd rather if he had won a Munster medal!'

The family though did pay a price for Niall's devotion to hurling. As a boy Niall always had a hurley in his hand. One famous day in Killarney Babs Keating scored a last-minute goal from a free. That was the day a mentor came on with a towel and was supposed to have switched the wet ball for a dry one to make it easier for Babs to score. Niall was about five at the time so he was practicing frees in the back garden after the match and his mother, Mary, was doing the ironing when the window was shattered to smithereens by Niall's sliotar. Mary nearly dropped dead with the shock of the shattering glass. All Niall said afterwards was, 'I was only doing Babs Keating!'

Ticking Clock

Niall always has a hurley in his car and is friendly with former hurlers like Nicky English. With time running out and Galway's victory apparently secure in the 1988 All-Ireland hurling final Nicky asked the referee how much time was left. The ever-helpful Slyvie Linnane butted in immediately to say, 'In your case a year and five minutes!'

Sausage-gate

When Nicky English became manager of Tipperary he was determined that he would leave no stone unturned until he got his team ready to claim the All-Ireland, which they did in 2001. Part of this punishing regime was the introduction of a Spartan diet. The results were immediate and spectacular throughout the squad, but there was one exception, Eugene O'Neill, whose weight remained unchanged. The Tipp management were baffled and summoned O'Neill for an interview. If O'Neill was hoping for a friendly chat he was shocked to discover that it was more in the style of the Spanish Inquisition before English and his entire management team. After a stubborn resistance initially O'Neill finally caved in and blurted out the one word that said so little but so much: 'Sausages.'

English was puzzled: 'What do you mean sausages?'

O'Neill replied: 'Well as you know Nicky I'm in college and when I get up in he morning the boys have sausages for me for breakfast. When I'm home during the day they stick on the pan and we have some more and then we have more in the evening. They're f**king killing me!'

LEGS AND CO.

Injuries can wreak havoc on a player. Given his injuries, Babs Keating once said to Nicky English, 'Nicky, if I had legs like yours, I'd be wearing nylons.' The one and only Babs is a man who knows all there is to know about the vagaries of hurling fortunes. He once said about management, 'It's a very short distance between a slap on the back and a kick in the arse!'

For his part Nicky English has known setbacks too: 'If I had ducks they'd drown.'

SPAT-GATE

During Babs Keating's 'second coming' as Tipperary manager, after a poor performance against Limerick, former Limerick manager Tom Ryan said that Babs was past his best. Keating was not going to take this comment on the chin. Instead, he went on Tipp FM and said: 'To me Tom Ryan is an ar**hole and has always been an ar**hole.'

SLIOTAR-GATE

Tipperary and Cork games during those years were noted for their skirmishes over sliotars. At the time the GAA had not imposed a standard sliotar for big matches – so most teams used the O'Neills models, whereas the Cork lads used the Cummins version. Cork were wont to try and break an advantage against Tipp by using that well-known Irish political tactic of playing 'cute hoors'.

When Tipperary got a close-in free, one of the Cork backs would start a bit of a row and one of his colleagues would smash the ball into the net as a gesture of solidarity. In the confusion the Cork goalie would puck-out the sliotar but having replaced it with a much older, heavier model, which would make it harder to strike with the kind of power that would yield a goal. Babs though quickly wised up to the tactic and famously went behind Dónal Óg Cusack's goal and drew the umpire's attention to the fuss, much to the annoyance of the Cork camp. The Cork rebels though had the last laugh; they countered Babs's monitoring of the situation in 2005 by cleverly selecting the oldest, deadest sliotar they could find and writing Tipp on it with a marker and holding it for when Tipperary got a penalty, then slipping it to Eoin Kelly and fooling him into thinking it was a Tipperary sliotar. When Kelly stood up though to take the shot he quickly realised the error of his ways because he was unable to get his customary velocity behind the shot and the penalty was saved.

ACHIEVEMENT IS IN THE EYE OF THE BEHOLDER

Michael Doyle had the virtually impossible task of succeeding Nicky English as Tipperary manager. One of his most courageous decisions was to take off star forward Eoin Kelly in a match against Galway. Kelly was being marked by the great Ollie Canning and was struggling. The Tipp fans though felt he should have been switched rather than replaced. Kelly though was phlegmatic: 'I did pretty well. I held Ollie to just a point.'

ALONE, ALL ALONE

Babs Keating once faced the problem of rallying his team, even though they were trailing at half-time by eight points. After a number of inspirational words in an effort to instil confidence Babs went around the team individually and asked each of them:

'Can we do it?'

To a man, they replied: 'We can. We can.'

He could feel the surge of belief invading the dressing room. Everything was going swimmingly until he turned to Joe Hayes and asked: 'Joe, can we do it?'

Joe took the wind out of his sails when he replied: 'It's not looking good.'

BABS-TALK

Babs has produced and been the subject of some classic quotes including:

If Babs Keating wrote a book on humility he'd be raging if it wasn't displayed in the shop window.

Offaly fan.

Babs Keating 'resigned' as coach because of illness and fatigue. The players were sick and tired of him.

Offaly fan.

Babs Keating has about as much personality as a tennis racket.

Offaly fan.

Babs Keating has been arrested in Nenagh for shaking a cigarette machine, but the Gardaí let him off when he said he only wanted to borrow twenty Players.

Waterford fan after Babs had predicted a heavy defeat for Waterford in the 2002 Munster final.

Babs himself has produced classic quotes like:

You can't win derbies with donkeys

Babs before Tipperary played Cork in the 1990 Munster final.
The Cork donkeys won.

Sheep in a heap.

Babs's description of the Offaly hurlers in 1998.

There's some fool texting me during matches – I hope he loses his phone for the rest of his life.

Babs after Tipp shocked Cork in 2007.

ODDS ON

There is a great book to be written on GAA rumours. After being held scoreless in the 2012 Munster final, in Tipperary the grapevine went into overdrive that Lar Corbett had bet on himself not to score in the game. As with many great rumours there was not a shred of truth in it. However, one of his teammates John O'Neill knocked some fun out of it when he shocked his teammates at a team meeting by saying Lar suffered from poor communication skills. As Lar documents in his autobiography, with every eye on him, O'Neill coolly informed Corbett that the next time he had a great tip for the Munster final he should share it with his teammates.

WHO WANTS TO BE A MILLIONAIRE?

Born at a very young age. I've never been a millionaire but I know I'd be unreal at it.

Tagline of Shane McGrath's Twitter account.

CHAPTER TWELVE

The Green and Red of Mayo

1951 was the last year Mayo reached the Holy Grail of winning the All-Ireland. More than in any other county they have experienced hurt, heartbreak and horror on big days in Croke Park. Yet as this chapter illustrates there is another side to Mayo football.

PICTURE THIS

When asked for a funny incident from his career Liam McHale provides a classic:

> We were staying in Maynooth College for the All-Ireland semifinal the day Princess Diana died. On the Sunday morning I was walking down into the breakfast room with PJ Loftus, who is a bit of a character. We were met at the door by the head priest, who is a very holy man.
>
> He said: 'Howya Liam. Howya PJ. Did you hear the awful news?'
>
> I immediately went into a panic because I feared that James Nallen or someone might be injured. He told us that Diana died.
>
> PJ Loftus replied: 'F**k off.'
>
> Me: 'How did she die?'
>
> The priest: 'She was killed in a car crash.'

PJ: 'F**k off.'
Me: 'What kind of crash was it?'
The priest: 'The paparazzi were chasing her.'
PJ: 'What the f**k was Pavarotti chasing her for?'
At that stage the priest said nothing and walked away in disgust!

HAY RAP

Will Galway bate Mayo
Not if they have Willie Joe?

The Saw Doctors.

Like the great John Joe O'Reilly, Willie Joe Padden is one of the elite group of footballers who have been immortalised in a song. The Mayo midfielder takes it all in his stride:

I know some of the lads in the band and sadly I think they chose me just because my named rhymed with Mayo not because of my brilliance on the pitch! There have been a few strange moments. Some years ago this American came over to visit Ireland just because he was a massive fan of the Saw Doctors and as soon as he came in the door of the bar I had in Castlebar at the time he asked me: 'Hey man, are you the guy in the song?'

With five Connacht medals and two All-Star awards to his name Padden can look back at the disappointments of the past with a wry smile:

When we played Kerry in the All-Ireland semi-final in 1981 we did well in the first half but they gave us such a hammering in the second half that our goalkeeper Michael Webb said to me: 'Every time I kicked out the ball I wondered would I have time to get back into the goal before the ball landed back in!'

IT'S JUST NOT CRICKET

Padden's quick wit was shown when he was approached by a stranger in an airport who said: 'You're a dead ringer for Ian Botham.' Quick as a flash Willie Joe replied: 'Funny I never get any of his cheques.'

NOTHING PERSONAL

Martin Carney lined out with Willie Joe in the Mayo colours, having previously played for his native Donegal. His strongest memory though is of playing in a Railway Cup match:

> I was playing corner-back for Connacht against Leinster in Ballinasloe and marking Johnny Mooney and the first ball that went in Johnny got a goal. Afterwards I couldn't understand why a section of the crowd were giving me terrible abuse and that continued for the rest of the game. I found out later that they were patients from the local psychiatric hospital who were let out for the day!

FAT LARRY

A cool temperament is a big help in sport. A classic example is the former Irish International Reggie Corrigan. When all around him were thrown into chaos when the floodlights failed during a Leinster match in the European Cup, plunging the ground into total darkness, Reggie calmly said, 'It's a bit dark isn't it?'

John O'Mahony is one of the coolest managers in the business. In 1989 Johno brought his native Mayo to the All-Ireland final. A teacher by profession, O'Mahony learned invaluable lessons from that defeat which stood him in good stead for his All-Ireland final win with Galway in 1998.

In the 1950s it was joked that there were just four lessons you needed to become a teacher in Ireland:

1. The history of Irish education was the hedge school.

2. Teaching Methods: always, always, always use a blackboard.

3. School Organisation: Never build a school beside an open sewer or dung hill.

4. Educational Psychology: Make sure to get the pupil outside the classroom before they wet the floor.

O'Mahony entered the teaching profession when thankfully a more sophisticated approach was called for. He was brilliant at getting into the head of individual players. When he managed Colm McGlynn who was a great full-forward but always liked to think he was a bit special. He told Johno that he could not train one evening.
'Why?'
'I have exams in College. I can't train Thursday either.'
'Why?'
'I have exams in College.'
'Well when are you free?'
'Ten o'clock on Wednesday night.'
'Okay I will meet you in Ringsend at 10 o'clock.'
Johno travelled all the way to Dublin and ran the sh*t* out of him. Colm never asked for special treatment again.

Battle of the Bulge

One of O'Mahony's key players in 1989 was Anthony 'Fat Larry' Finnerty, who was one of the great characters of Mayo football. He was fat in the winter but lost a lot of weight in the summer. Three days after Mayo lost the All-Ireland final to Cork in 1989 everyone was very down in his local pub, Mitchell's. Anthony had scored a goal in the game that had brought Mayo back into the match but missed a goal chance late in the game, which might have turned the game for the Westerners. Someone asked him to say a few words to cheer them up. Anthony said, 'If I had got that goal I missed ye'd have been talking about me all winter but now that I missed it ye'll never stop talking about me.'

WET, WET, WET

During Brian McDonald's controversial tenure as trainer of Mayo, the former Dublin player was taking a training session and twenty-three or twenty-four players were jogging around the pitch. He told them that if every time he blew his whistle they were to jump high in the air and imagine they were catching a famous ball. This drill went on until they got level with the dressing room when Finnerty started to zoom towards the dressing room. The irate trainer shouted at him, 'Where are you going?'

Fat Larry replied, 'I'm just going in to get my gloves. That bloody ball you want us to catch is awful slippy!'

AT A PUSH

Pat Spillane has a unique take on the McDonald controversy:

I often think of what would have happened if Mayo went on to win the All-Ireland in 1992. They came within a whisker of beating the eventual All-Ireland champions Donegal in the All-Ireland semi-final. In a highly-publicised saga afterwards, the Mayo players signed a petition which called for the removal of their manager Brian McDonald and in the process released a list of training methods which they had used during the year which seemed to border on the farcical. Only one side of the story was told in public. Player power saw McDonald bowing out with Jack O'Shea taking his place, only for Mayo to be absolutely massacred by Cork the following year in the All-

Ireland semi-final. With a bit of luck though Mayo could easily have beaten Donegal in 1992 and who knows what would have happened against Dublin in the All-Ireland final. McDonald, being very cute, improvised when there was no field available for training by getting the Mayo lads to push cars around the car park. If Mayo won that All-Ireland everyone would have said McDonald was a genius and car-pushing would have become part of the training manual for every team in the country.

Crime and Punishment

TJ Kilgallon was one of the chief car-pushers on that evening in Dunnes Stores car park in Castlebar. He has many happy memories to treasure of his colleagues in the green and red:

> One incident probably sums up the tight bond we had. We went for a holiday trip to the Canaries and one night Jimmy Burke was in a nightclub when a guy stole his wallet and ran outside with Jimmy chasing after him. Three of us happened to be coming in the opposite direction and we chased the thief into an alley. I'm six foot two but I was the smallest of our foursome. The guy had no escape and turned very contrite and handed the wallet back saying: 'Your wallet, sir.' Let's just say it wasn't left at that!

Book him Danno

During his career TJ witnessed some bizarre events:

> We were playing Galway in the Connacht championship when Tomás Tierney 'did a job' on Kevin McStay. Kevin was badly injured and had to go off. I was friends with Tomás and had shared a house with him at one stage but I couldn't believe that the referee, Seán Mullaney from Roscommon, wasn't booking

him. I confronted Seán about it and he told me that the reason was that he had lost his notebook and couldn't book Tomás without it!

CAN'T GET NO SATISFACTION

Around that time Mayo went on a team holiday to Florida and discovered that the Rolling Stones were in concert there. The Mayo management asked one of the lads if he would like to see them play and he asked in all seriousness: who are they playing?

HE'S GOT LEGS AND HE KNOWS HOW TO USE THEM

Only a late bounce of the ball deprived John Maughan of managing Mayo to an All-Ireland title in 1996. Maughan was famous for always wearing his togs on the sideline. Hence the comment: 'John Maughan belongs to the GLE club – the greatest legs ever.'

HOW THE WEST WAS LOST

After the 1996 and 1997 All-Irelands when Mayo let All-Ireland titles slip through their fingers Pat Spillane poured scorn on the Mayo forwards in particular. When the county's ladies team started winning All-Irelands and Cora Staunton emerged as a national figure Spillane deftly used their success as a rod to beat the men's team with: 'The time has come for me to confound my critics and bravely admit that in the last five years Mayo have had one of the best teams I have ever seen – their ladies football team. I can now exclusively reveal that plans are well advanced for my new series about Mayo footballers. It is to be called *Footballer's Husbands*.'

BRIEF ENCOUNTERS

Mayo have a great tradition of producing top-class characters and players. It has become a cliché for journalists and broadcasters to refer to a particular player's 'cultured left foot'. Yet every cliché has its truth and from the days when he first sprang to prominence with St Jarlath's College, Tuam, where he won All-Ireland College's senior medals in both 1960 and 1961, there was never any doubt that John Morley's left foot merited this soubriquet. John was always getting slagged about his right leg but he always defended it by saying that without it he couldn't use his left!

The most famous incident in his illustrious career came in the 1970 League final clash when Mayo defeated Down. John was playing at half-back, when a Down player grabbed him and tore his shorts. Just as he was about to put his foot into a new pair of shorts, the ball came close by, he abandoned his shorts and in his briefs fielded the ball and cleared it heroically down the field to the adulation of the crowd.

FRUSTRATION

Paddy Prendergast was the full-back when Mayo won back-to-back All-Irelands in 1950 and 1951. His team was normally very assiduous in its preparation:

> We had great characters in the team. John Forde was very serious. When we stayed in Mrs Gaughan's guesthouse our routine was to go for a ten-mile walk after breakfast. Before a big game against Kerry Tom Langan said he was going to skip the walk that day because his stomach wasn't too good. Then Mick Flanagan said he would not go either because his leg wasn't too good. John jumped up and said: 'For Jaysus sake, wire Kerry and award them the game!'

THE BRADY BUNCH

David Brady is probably as famous now for one comment as his years of fine performances in the Mayo jersey: 'Every man, woman and monkey is nearly writing them off in Mayo.'

PERENNIAL PROBLEMS

Mayo's old failings, like Kildare's, in the forwards department were once again exposed in the 2013 national semi-finals. This led Malachy Clerkin to observe in the *Irish Times*: 'Mayo and Kildare will be the dog against most teams but will likely find one to make them the lamp post the nearer we get to September.'

CHAPTER THIRTEEN

Where We Sported and Played

Hurling heroes have to be truly exceptional to be recognised in Cork. One hurler who gained iconic status on Leeside was the late Jack Lynch. He took mischievous pleasure in recalling Frank O'Connor's claim that Cork had a mental age of seventeen. You had to leave at seventeen if you were to be happy and stimulated whereas Dublin had a mental age of twenty-one. In the early days of the revival of Cork's inter-county hurling fortunes, the late thirties and early forties, Lynch had many an argument with his teammates as to why Cork did not do better in a particular game. Whenever things got particularly heated Bobby Ryng, of Carrigtwohill, a forward who had a stammer used to intervene with 'no p-p-p-politics here'. Of course politics then was the least of their problems but Bobby used the tactic to completely diffuse the situation.

Lynch had a famous altercation with Tony Reddin, the legendary Tipperary goalkeeper. Reddin had something of a speech impediment. During the white heat of a Cork–Tipp clash Lynch charged into Reddin and in the process bundled both of them into the net. An irate Reddin roared, 'F-f-f-f**k you Lynch. Try that again an' there'll be a f-f-f-f**king by-election.'

LATE ARRIVAL

Lynch won five All-Ireland hurling medals with Cork. He also won an All-Ireland football medal. His football career left him with one enduring memory from the 1945 All-Ireland football final. Having completed his law examinations he was in digs on the southside of Dublin in Rathgar. He met the Cork team at 'Kingsbridge' Station on the Saturday evening and he told the selection committee he would not be at the hotel the next morning as there was a bus route near his digs which passed by Croke Park and that he would go straight to the stadium. He was waiting in a queue about twenty yards long. Bus after bus passed, each taking only a couple of people at a time. At one stage Lynch barged to the head of the queue. The conductor told him to go back and await his turn. He pointed to his bag of 'togs' and said he was playing in the All-Ireland football final in Croke Park within the hour. The conductor said sarcastically that this was the best reason for breaking a queue that he ever heard but let him stay on. He alighted from the bus at the junction of the Drumcondra and Conyngham Roads, and ran around to the back of the Cusack Stand where the dressing rooms were then located. He knocked at the Cork dressing room door to be greeted by an ominous silence except the sound of footsteps slowly and deliberately pacing the floor and this within only about fifteen minutes from the throw-in. The door opened. It was Jim Hurley, formerly Cork hurling midfielder, then Secretary of UCC and chairman of the Cork Selection Committee. Lynch expected to be 'bawled' out. Instead he got, 'Hello Jack Lynch, you were great to come.'

AN EDUCATION

As a pupil at the famous North Mon, Lynch had a keen appreciation for the role of the Christian Brothers in Irish life generally, but in the promotion of hurling in particular. He especially admired their commitment and the commitment they inspired in others. He once told the story of a clever little boy at an expensive and liberal private school who was underachieving badly, particularly in Maths, so the parents, devout atheists, sent him to a very strict Christian Brothers establishment. He returned after the first day, tiny schoolbag brimming with books, and locked himself in his room for three hours with his homework. This went on for a few weeks and at the end of his first month he returned with his interim report card, which showed that he was first in his class in Maths. His delighted parents asked what had awakened his drive and he said, a bit grimly, 'I knew that it was a serious subject when they showed me the guy nailed to the plus sign!'

IN SOLIDARITY

One of the people who followed Jack Lynch into the Taoiseach's office was Garret Fitzgerald, who was not known for his interest in hurling. His lack of hurling knowledge was most graphically illustrated on a trip to Cork. He became Taoiseach in 1981 at the height of an economic crisis and with the hunger strikes at their height in the North. At a time of turbulence at home one of the few good news stories was the collapse of communism in Poland. The fact that everybody knew Pope John Paul II was involved added to the interest in the story – as he had famously visited Ireland two years previously. Poland was gaining its freedom largely because of the efforts of the trade union Solidarity. Everyone in Ireland at the time knew that the Solidarity colours were red and white. Garret arrived in Cork on a Sunday and saw hordes of people swathed in red and white, and was very impressed at such political activism, not realising that they were on their way to a Munster championship match. Garret is said to have turned to his aide and said, 'I never knew Solidarity had such popular support in Cork.'

On the canvas trail in 1981 when he posed for a photo opportunity, swinging a hurley, Garret allegedly said to a journalist, 'I've always wanted to play hurling so I thought it would be a good thing to learn the rudiments of the game.'

His interviewer asked, 'So have you learned much?'

Garret replied, 'Yes I have. How to swing a cue.'

Lord of the Rings

On Cork hurling's roll of honour pride of place goes to Christy Ring. In 1944 Limerick drew with Cork in the Munster championship. In the replay the Shannonsiders led by five points with fifteen minutes to go as Mick Mackey scored a goal only to see it disallowed because the referee had blown for an infringement on him. To add insult to injury Limerick spurned a scoring opportunity from the free in. Cork pegged back the lead to draw level and in the dying seconds the wizard of Cloyne struck. Never were truer words spoken:

> Now Cork is bate,
> the hay is saved,
> the thousands wildly sing.
> They speak too soon,
> my sweet garsun,
> 'cos here comes Christy Ring.

Cork had won the three previous All-Irelands and were bidding to become the first side to win the four-in-a-row. Ring's brother, Willie John, ran in from the sideline to tell Christy, 'If you get the ball into your hand run with it because your man's legs are gone.' Seconds later Ring got the ball and made a forty yard solo run, which has become part of hurling legend, before unleashing a powerful shot for the decisive goal. After the match Willie John asked Christy why he had not gone for safety and taken a point.

Ring replied, 'That would be too easy. Anyone could have scored a point.'

For years and years Ring wreaked havoc on Tipperary hurlers. The great Tipp star Mick 'Rattler' Byrne said to him at one stage, 'By God, Christy, we'll have to shoot you.'

Ring calmly replied, 'Ye might as well. Ye've tried everything else.'

PARROT SYNDROME

In the 1950s a Cork hurler was greeted at the end of a disappointing performance in a Munster championship match with the frank appraisal of one Cork fan, 'That was the worst display I ever saw by a Cork player. You were complete rubbish. In fact you were even worse.'

The hurler, quite disturbed, informed Christy Ring what the man had said. Ring replied, 'That poor chap is not really responsible for what he says. He never has an original thought. He just goes around repeating what everybody else is saying!'

LOW OPINION

Ring once met a young journalist on his way into an All-Ireland final. The journalist was trying to get information from him but Christy was more enigmatic than the Dead Sea Scrolls. Eventually the journalist lost patience and decided to quit while he still retained a shred of dignity and asked Christy one final question. 'Can you tell me where to go for the press box?'

'To hell and back,' Christy replied.

I Don't Like Mondays

Another time Christy was asked his opinion of an up-and-coming star in Cork hurling who regularly boasted about his sporting prowess. Christy said, 'On his day Charlie is the best hurler in the world. Unfortunately his day is always a Monday!'

Christy was famous for his commitment to training. One story that has gone into legend dates back to the time his wife gave birth to their first son. A few hours later Christy was said to have been on his way to training when he was greeted and warmly congratulated by a neighbour. When she saw his gear and hurley she said, 'I'm surprised to see you training just after your wife gave birth to your son.'

Christy coolly replied, 'I don't care if 'twas a young bonham she had. I'm not going to miss training.'

Ring was very single-minded and once instructed a debutante on the Cork team to 'always keep your eye on the ball – even when it's in the referee's pocket'.

Pride and Prejudice

One man does not make a hurling team, though Ring had his doubts. One Sunday he was jumping over the stile instead of displaying his pass as he went into a match. An irate County Board official, a former teammate of Ring's, caustically inquired where was the wizard of Cloyne's pass.

'I don't have it.'

'But Christy, you ought to have. You won no less than eight All-Ireland medals.'

The reply was fast and devastating: 'And if I hadn't been carrying passengers like you, I'd have won at least eight more!'

TROUBLEMAKERS

Christy and a friend attended a seminar on coaching in a church hall in Cork one evening. The priest approached the great man apologetically and said, 'There are very bad acoustics here.'

Christy's friend replied reassuringly, 'Don't worry Father. I'm not sure who these acoustics are but if they start any trouble we'll throw them out.'

GAME OF THRONES

Another story relates to the three Mcs: Gerald, Justin and Charlie McCarthy. The night before an All-Ireland final they were supposed to be tucked up in their beds for a night. The three young men decided to take a trip into the city centre to sample the atmosphere. The problem was that it was much harder for them to get a taxi back to the team hotel. Two of the team mentors Jim 'Tough' Barry and Donie Keane were patrolling the corridor. The three lads knew they would be read the riot act so they hid until the coast was clear and they raced up the stairs and into their beds. Within moments there was a rap on the door. The three amigos pretended they were fast asleep. Then came a louder rap they could not possibly ignore and the question, 'What were ye lads up to?'

'We're in bed.'

'Open the door.'

Charlie McCarthy nonchalantly walked to the door, pretending to rub the sleep from his eyes as he let the two mentors in, 'What's the problem, Jim? We were fast asleep.'

Jim looked at him with steely eyes, 'Is that so? Jaysus, Charlie you're the only man I know to wear a collar and tie in bed.'

THE FRIDAY FAST

Like Liam Griffin, Justin McCarthy is one of the great evangelists of the game: 'Hurling identifies my Irishness. I'm not an Irish speaker, so the game portrays my national identity.'

The late RTÉ GAA Correspondent Mick Dunne was an admirer of McCarthy's:

> He was very committed to everything he did and left nothing to chance. It was a very different time during his playing days. In 1966 he deservedly won the Texaco Hurler of the Year award. The morning after the reception where he had been presented with his award, Justin celebrated in style – by having a massive fry-up for breakfast. The problem was that in those days Catholics were not allowed to eat meat on Fridays, with the result that fish was on the menu in most Irish homes. When Justin realised the terrible sin he had committed he went to his priest for absolution!

BE AFRAID ... BE VERY AFRAID!

The Cork County Board seems to favour austere personalities. It is interesting to note that they appointed Donal O'Grady as their hurling manager. I enjoyed Keith Duggan's comment in the *Irish Times* in September, 2003: 'When Donal O'Grady smiles you can hear the cello in Jaws.'

MURPHY'S LAW

For years Frank Murphy has been inextricably linked with Cork GAA. One of Frank's finest hours came in 1983 after the football Munster final. Jack O'Shea was the Kerry captain that day and Micheál Ó Muircheartaigh was training Jacko and the Kerry lads in Dublin at the time. Kerry had won the Munster final every year from 1975 and in 1983 so most people expected them to win again. Jacko worked on his victory speech with Ó Muircheartaigh and they were very happy with it. The only problem was that Kerry lost the match. Jacko's great speech was never made.

There was another twist to the story. Kerry forgot to bring the Munster Cup with them and it was only quick thinking by Frank Murphy that saved the day. He searched a press in the back room and found some cup – apparently the Cork junior championship trophy. That's the Cup that was presented to the Cork captain, Christy Ryan, but nobody seemed to notice.

Hanging on the Telephone

Cork dramatically won that match courtesy of a sensational last-minute goal from Tadhg Murphy. Cork full-back Kevin Kehilly rang Murphy a few days later only to be told, 'I'm sorry Kevin I can't talk to you now 'cos I've somebody with me. Ring me back in ten minutes.' He did and when he rang he got Murphy's answering machine. The message was, 'This is Tadhgie Murphy here, the Man with the Golden Boot. Kevin, without me you wouldn't have won a Munster medal.'

Old Age and Failing Powers

Throughout Kehilly's career his Cork colleagues always kept him in laughs. The autumn of his inter-county football career was the era of the roving full-forward. He was the last of the traditional full-backs who marshalled the square and it was a big culture shock for him to have to start running half way out the field and running back in again for the whole match and it was tough on his aging body. Billy Morgan was always winding him up before a match saying, 'Kevin keep close to the goal today. I didn't bring any oxygen!'

THE YOUNG ONES

Kehilly's inter-county career had ended in 1989 when Cork regained the All-Ireland. Among the Cork stars of that team was John Cleary, a very accurate forward, though not the biggest man in the world. Before one of Cork's clashes with Kerry Jack O'Shea came up to him and, in an effort to psyche him out, said, 'You're too small and too young for a game like this.' Cleary said nothing until after the game when Cork emerged triumphant and as he walked off the pitch past Jacko he softly said, 'You're too old for a game like this.'

PUTTING OFF THE INEVITABLE

In the glory days of the Kerry team Cleary told the story of when Cork trailed Kerry by 2–19 to 0–5 at half-time. Kerry were to play with a gale force wind in the second half. So desperate were the Cork mentors in the dressing room at half-time that they asked the tea lady if she had any advice for them. After pausing for thought she said: 'If ye want to prolong ye'er stay in the championship the only thing ye can do is stay as long as ye possibly can here in the dressing room.'

STYLE COUNCIL

Not surprisingly Pat Spillane has strong memories about Cork footballers:

> I gave a talk at the Jurys Sportstar of the Year awards; talk about meeting the enemies. Niall Cahalane was in the audience. He was probably the most difficult player I ever marked. I told the crowd that Niall had such a love of the Kerry jersey that he used to collect bits and pieces of it by marking me so closely, all through the years.

FINDING NEMO

Billy Morgan had a great reputation as a player and manager with Nemo Rangers. It is said that he loves Cork but would die for Nemo Rangers. When Morgan was manager of Cork he employed two psychologists to get the team in the right frame of mind before playing a Munster final against Kerry. The first guy had the job of calming the team down. Everyone had to close their eyes and picture themselves walking along a riverbank on a summer's evening with butterflies were fluttering; the smell of freshly-mown grass and the sounds of birds singing nearby. They had to imagine walking up a little path on a hill with a cabin at the top, walking into the cabin, sitting down and feeling at peace.

The second pyschologist had the job of getting the team all fired up and he left them ready to play out of their skins when they got out on the pitch. The Cork team left the dressing room with the sound of Tina Turner singing 'Simply the Best' ringing in their ears. What happened? Kerry hammered the living daylights out of them that year.

AN UNKNOWN QUALITY

Another year after Linford Christie won the gold medal in the Olympics the mantra in the Cork dressing room was that the Cork team should take inspiration from Linford Christie. For ten minutes the team had the virtues of Linford extolled to them. When the inspirational words were finished a very prominent Cork player turned to another and whispered in all sincerity in a bewildered tone: 'Who the f**k is Linford Christie?'

ANONYMOUS

Dinny Allen was the only the Cork player to be chosen on the Centenary Team of players to never have won an All-Ireland in 1984. Five years later he put that omission to right when he captained the Cork team to win the All-Ireland. A lot of hurlers on the ditch alleged that Allen had not contributed much to winning Sam. As a result Dinny christened himself the 'non-playing captain'!

Them and Us

Who has the most loyal supporters? There has always been a great rivalry between Cork and Kerry fans.

A Kerry fan goes up to heaven and he is very surprised to see that St Peter is wearing a Cork jersey. 'Why should I let you in here?' asked St Peter. The Kerry fan replied: 'Well last month I gave a hundred euro to the St Vincent de Paul. Last week I gave sixty euro to Focus Ireland. Yesterday I gave forty euro to Trocaire.'

St Peter replied, 'I'm not sure if we want a Kerry fan in heaven but seeing as you gave generously to charity wait here and I'll check out with God what he thinks of your situation.'

St Peter came back a few minutes later and said: 'God agrees with me. Here's your two hundred euro. Now f**k off out of here.'

CHAPTER FOURTEEN

Seasons of Sundays

Sex, the Italians say, is the poor man's opera. That is utter nonsense. Anyone with half a brain knows that gaelic games is the poor man's opera.

It is because of this that the media are so important in the GAA. The role of the media is simultaneously to inform, educate, enlighten and entertain. Sometimes the football journalists manage all four at once, notably the *Sunday Times'* headline announcing the replay date after Arsenal and Sheffield Wednesday drew in the 1993 FA Cup final: 'Arsenal, Wednesday, Thursday.'

Often the media are at their most entertaining when they are putting the boot in such as *The Sun*'s malicious verdict on the Intertoto Cup: 'The InterTwobob Cup.'

From time to time the print media betray their ignorance of their beautiful game: 'Commodore already sponsors Tessa Sanderson, Chelsea FC and a football team, Bayern Munich.'

While the media may aim for enlightenment, they sometimes create confusion.

John Inverdale: 'What do you think the score will be?'
Caller to Five Live: 'Nil-all draw.'
'So who'll score for Everton then?'

In the light of such incisive analysis it is perhaps not surprising that Roy Keane is so dismissive of football pundits: 'I wouldn't listen to these people in the pub and yet they're on TV. I've done it once. Never again. I'd rather go to the dentist! I wouldn't trust some of these people to walk my dog.'

Nonetheless for their services to the entertainment industry this chapter pays homage to the GAA's Fourth Estate.

JUST ANOTHER MANIC SUNDAY

1979 will be forever remembered as the year the Pope came to Ireland. It also marked the first transmission of *The Sunday Game,* a rare programme then devoted exclusively to gaelic games. Popular Galway-based journalist Jim Carney and the late Seán Óg Ó Ceallacháin were the first presenters. Seán Óg's contribution to gaelic games is well known because of his varied career as a Dublin county footballer and hurler, referee and sports commentator and reporter. In fact so associated is he in the popular mind with gaelic games that people had great difficulty thinking that he had an interest in any other sports. This was memorably demonstrated when a caller to RTÉ Radio Sport rang to ask about Manchester United. The conversation went as follows:

'Is this Seán Óg?'
'It is indeed.'
'Seán Óg Ó Ceallacháin?'
'The one and the same?'
'Off the radio?'
'That's me!'
'Sure what the f**k would you know about soccer?'

DUNNE AND DUSTED

A great champion of hurling was the late Mick Dunne, father of newsreader Eileen. In 1949 Mick joined the *Irish Press* as junior librarian before quickly graduating to and becoming a gaelic games correspondent and later Gaelic Games Editor of the Sports Department.

Once sat in a hotel having his breakfast the morning after a Munster final and two tables away he could hear two men dissecting his report on the match. Their remarks were not very complimentary. Later that morning he stopped for petrol at a small shop outside Thurles. As Tipperary had lost heavily the previous day the shopkeeper was still in foul humour. He asked Mick if he had been at the match. When Mick replied in the affirmative the shopkeeper went into a lengthy analysis of why Tipperary lost and then proceeded to ask Mick if he had seen, 'what that f**king bast**d Mick Dunne had written in the *Irish Press*?' When Mick politely replied that he was aware of the contents of the article the shopkeeper launched into a vicious tirade about Mick's knowledge of hurling and cast a number of doubts on his parentage in the process. Mick made no response until the very end when the shopkeeper said, 'I bet that fella's getting a fortune for writing that rubbish. Tell you what, although I hate him I wish I had his money.'

Mick calmly paid him for the petrol and said, 'Well you've just got £5 of it.'

THE NUMBERS GAME

Mick was one of the journalists involved in selecting the team that would travel to New York to play in the Cardinal Cushing Games. It was almost the precursor of the All-Stars. They tried especially to pick some good players from the weaker counties. The importance of picking players from the weaker countries led them to speak about the terms of reference in selection decisions. One of their number blurted out immediately, 'Let's pick the team first and we'll sort out the terms of reference later!'

JIMMY'S COMMENTATING ON MATCHES

A bit of humour is great in a presenter or analyst. That's why someone like Des Lynam was so popular. He's got some great one-liners like: 'There's Frank Leboeuf and his son – Le Spare Rib.' His best though was probably: 'Our experts tonight are two guys who between them have won 106 caps for Scotland. Kenny Dalglish who has won 104 and Bob Wilson who has won two.'

However, the award for the all-time best quote has to go to the great Jimmy Magee's remark that: 'Brazil – they're so good it's like they are running around the pitch playing with themselves.'

Jimmy is one of Ireland's best-loved personalities. In that much overused phrase he is a national institution. Jimmy got a major scoop at his first Olympics in 1972 in Munich, where he was the first journalist to report on the taking hostage of eleven Israeli athletes. Magee is no less a diplomat than a great broadcaster. He has a great flair for handling Dublin fans. 'Jimmy,' an anxious Dublin fan desperately seeking assurance before the replay against Meath in 2007 said, 'do you think we still have a great team?'

'Ah, my good man,' Jimmy replied with the utmost sincerity, '"Great" is not the word to describe it!'

EYE OF THE TIGER

As the whole world knows Tiger Woods is partial to female company. He seems to think Jimmy is a kindred spirit. In 1997 when Tiger put himself on golf's map of greats by winning his first Masters Jimmy was one of several hundred journalists outside the media tent hoping to get a few words with the new superstar. Jimmy noticed Tiger's mother and went over and chatted to her about her son's great future. After a time Tiger came out to meet up with his mother. She greeted him: 'Eldrick [his real name], I want you to meet my friend from Ireland. This is Jimmy. He's been keeping me company all afternoon.'

In the frenzied press conference that followed when Jimmy asked Tiger a question, he ambiguously replied: 'And here's the man who kept my mother company!'

WISH YOU WERE HERE

One of the most magical moments in Irish sporting history was Ireland's win over England 1–0 in Germany in Euro '88. Jimmy met four Irish fans the next day in Cologne looking 'tired and emotional'. He was a bit bemused because the match had taken place four hundred kilometres away in Stuttgart. When they saw Jimmy one shouted across at him: 'You're the Memory Man, right? You know everything, right?'

'I am indeed. What do you want to know?'

'Where's our bleedin' hotel?'

HOMEWARD BOUND

Despite his interest in other sports, gaelic games are Jimmy's first love. It was listening to the wireless commentary of the famous 1947 All-Ireland final between Kerry and Cavan in New York, the only one ever to be played outside Ireland, that the twelve-year-old boy first dreamed of becoming a commentator. One of his great heroes is Christy Ring, a friendship cemented during their involvement in the Jimmy Magee All-Stars, which raised over six million euro for various charities down through the years.

Ring was not above putting Jimmy in his place. During one match for the All-Stars when Magee was not showing much mobility Ring barked at him from the sideline: 'Did you find it yet Jimmy?'

'What's that Christy?'

'The thing you're looking for. You're running around the same spot, Jimmy. You haven't moved out of it.'

On one occasion the motley crew of the Magee All-Stars played a match in New York. Before playing the team were watching a softball game and they were asked to try out this strange game. It was decided that Ring should be the team's representative. The Cork legend though feigned ignorance to his hosts. 'Give me that there what-do-you-call-it. Is that a bat or a stick, or what do you call it?'

After he was told it was a bat he inquired with a puzzled tone. 'Now do you hold it like this or like that?'

After being shown how to hold the bat he asked them to provide their best pitcher. When an athletic young man appeared he gave a mighty effort but Ring hit the ball into the stratosphere and out of the stadium. All the softball players looked at him in shock and awe. Ring nonchalantly said: 'That's a home run now, isn't it?'

LOST IN TRANSLATION

Jimmy had a few mishaps in his broadcasting career. A caller on his radio show rang in with a question. The only problem was that he started speaking in Irish and Jimmy's Irish was not up to a conversation with a fluent Gaelic speaker on the national airwaves. He knew he had to say something so as not to appear rude or ignorant, so he said, *'Agus ainm?'*

The reply was, *'Seán.'*

Jimmy didn't know what 'address' was in Irish, so he asked *'As Corcaigh?'*

The reply was: *'Ní hea, as Luimneach.'*

Then the caller asked a question, but Jimmy hadn't a clue what he was saying. Thinking on his feet, Jimmy started saying, 'Hello! Seán? Seán? … We seem to have lost him there …'

Seán was saying, 'No, you haven't! I'm here.'

Jimmy shot him down: 'No, we've lost Seán. We'll try him again.' So he took him off the air, because he could think of no other way of getting out of it.

THE FRENCH CONNECTION

Jimmy is also famous for his coverage of the Tour de France. At the 1987 tour he went to the cyclists' medical area when he heard they had a new laser treatment as he had a sore leg. When he emerged, he found four waiting cyclists, one of whom was Seán Kelly, who said: 'So, you're the man who is holding us up. That's gas, we're riding in the Tour de France and Magee is in the tent!'

ME AND JIMMY MAGEE

My love of sport nearly cost me my family. They say confession is good for the soul. I hope so. For over thirty years I have harboured a dark secret from my nearest and dearest. Many's the sleepless night I have turned and twisted in my bed as the pangs of guilt racked my troubled conscience. No amount of counting sheep could shake off the tidal waves of remorse that swept over me.

In my defence it wasn't really my fault. The real villain was Jimmy Magee. The great sports commentators share a magical capacity to raise and refresh the spirit and to heighten the quality of human perception. Jimmy is one of them. His is a world of wonder, admiration and enchantment. He is the exception to Alexander Pope's rule, 'Words are like leaves; and where they most abound, much fruit of sense beneath is rarely found.'

It was FA Cup final day in 1979 and my only worry was if Liam Brady would lead Arsenal to triumph over Manchester United. My family though were in a tizzy because my aunt Sheila was getting married two days later after a twelve-year courtship. Nobody could accuse her of marrying in haste. The match had thankfully permitted me to provide a pretext for missing the rehearsal. All I had to do was to deposit the newly-acquired three-tiered wedding cake into my uncle-in-law-to-be's car, for safe transportation to the hotel, while the rest of the family went to the church.

With five minutes to go Arsenal were cruising with a 2–0 lead and Jimmy assured me that the Cup was theirs. This was the moment to leave out the cake.

It was starting to rain. The rain slid, tapping, through the branches, and swept in windy puffs across the fields. As I carefully placed the cake on the back seat of the capri I could hear Jimmy recklessly abandoning his normal calm, mellifluous tones for a state of near frenzy. I raced back inside to see that United had scored. Jimmy could scarcely contain his excitement. A minute later United equalised. Jimmy's voice pulsated with enthusiasm. Then with time almost up Chippy Brady produced another piece of wizardry to sensationally set up the winning goal. By now Jimmy was in a state of near mystical rapture.

As the Cup was presented a feeling of panic descended on me. I raced outside. My worst fears were realised. I had left the car door open and our dog – imaginatively called Lassie – was licking the wedding cake.

Lassie was warm, brown and smooth-coated, with a cream arrow on her forehead and flecks of cream on her two front feet. She was a very knowing, friendly creature and I loved her with a passion. At that moment I could have killed her, especially as icing dripped off her whiskers like a snowman melting in a heatwave.

The damage to the cake was surprisingly small and a little surgery with a knife seemed to do the trick. Blood may be thicker than water, but it is also a great deal nastier. I decided that news of Lassie's appreciation for the wedding cake was best kept to myself. Whoever said silence is golden knew what they were talking about.

Such was my acute anxiety that overnight I was attacked by a virulent form of acne. My mother thought that was the reason that during the wedding I sought the shadows as resolutely as the Phantom of the Opera.

A look of adoration passed into my aunt's face as she cut the cake, like the look of the mother of a child who has just won first prize. To my eyes the icing looked as buttery and soft as white custard. So acute was the sensation of panic across my chest I felt I might explode.

Everyone agreed they had never tasted nicer wedding cake.

Questions and Answers

Post-match interviews are fraught with pitfalls. Witness Nicolas Colsaerts's response to Sky Sports request to sum up his Ryder Cup experiences: 'There are no tools you can use out there. You've just got to go with what you have in your pants.'

Then there was Tracy Piggott's infamous interview with horse trainer Peter Casey after Flemenstar won in Leopardstown in January 2012. To say the seventy-something-year-old was happy is an understatement: 'I can't believe it, I can't believe it. I'll have f**king sex tonight and everything.'

Closing Time

Injury meant that the late Roscommon star Brendan Lynch's career ended prematurely after another Connacht title victory in 1952. His work as a garda superintendent continued to bring him into contact with some famous GAA figures:

In my first week I found myself prosecuting a man for a drunk-driving charge. He called a number of character witnesses. The first was six foot four, was wearing no shirt but instead Wellingtons and an overcoat. I then checked his name. It was

Con Houlihan. In his cross-examination he was asked: 'Do you take a drink yourself?'

'In a social capacity?'

'How much would you drink?'

'Not too much … Ten or twelve pints at the one sitting.'

The next time I met him was in O'Connell Street. He was wearing runners. I wouldn't mind if it was a pair but he was wearing two odd ones!

CLASSICS

Con Houlihan had a phrase for every occasion. Here is my fab four:

1. *On bad grammar:* A man who will misuse an apostrophe is capable of anything.

2. *On a fellow journalist:* There he is, poor fella, forgotten but not gone.

3. *On Italia '90:* I missed Italia '90, I was in Italy at the time.

4. *On Paddy Cullen's frantic effort to keep the ball out before Mike Sheehy's famous goal in the 1978 All-Ireland final:* He was like a woman who smells a cake burning.

WHO SAID WHAT?

Dermot Earley won All-Stars in 1974 and 1979 and a National League medal in 1979 but unusually found himself embroiled in controversy in 1977 in the All-Ireland semi-final against Roscommon. With the score tied at Armagh 3–9 Roscommon 2–12 as Earley faced up to a long-distance free, the last kick of the game, Gerry O'Neill (brother of former Celtic manager, Martin), the

Armagh trainer, ran across the field in front of him and shouted something at him. The kick sailed high and wide. There was much press comment on the O'Neill–Earley incident in the following days. In his column in the *Evening Press* Con Houlihan offered two All-Ireland tickets to the person who could tell him what O'Neill said to Earley.

MEEJAH MOMENTS

Inevitably pundits and the Fourth Estate have their quota of quotable quotes:

Gaelic football is like a love affair: if you don't take it seriously, it's no fun; if you do take it seriously, it breaks your heart.

Patrick Kavanagh.

Is the ref going to blow his whistle? No, he's going to blow his nose.

Commentator on Kilkenny FM.

Frank [The Cork County Secretary] Murphy: The comb-over who rules the world.

Tom Humphries.

The ruin has rained the game.

Jimmy Smyth.

Mayo have more baggage than a hotel concierge.

Damian Lawlor.

FLOAT LIKE A BUTTERFLY, STING LIKE A BEE

One of Ireland's biggest ever sporting occasions was held in GAA Headquarters. On 19 July, 1972 it took Muhammad Ali eleven rounds to defeat Al 'Blue' Lewis at Croke Park. The fight itself was unremarkable but it was a wonderful occasion, particularly after Ali announced that his maternal great-grandfather Abe Grady had emigrated from Clare over a century before. As part of the build-up to the fight Ali met the Taoiseach, Jack Lynch, who informed the pugilist that despite his busy schedule he hoped to make it to the fight the following Wednesday. Ali replied, 'Since you're a busy man, I guess I'll get it over quickly.'

'Ah sure, that would spoil it.'

'Well in that case, I'll let Lewis stay in the ring for more than one round.'

'I might get in there for a few rounds myself and keep things going,' said Jack.

Ali's press conferences before the fight were never less than memorable. At one point he caught the journalists on the hop when out of the blue he asked, 'What were the last words the Lord uttered at the Last Supper?'

There was silence as the hacks present were not known for their theological expertise. Ali answered his own question, 'Let every man pick up his own cheque.'

Although the fight itself did not live up to the frenzied anticipation it created one journalist was heard to remark, 'After this performance all we can do is rename the place Muhammad Alley.'

ALL PUNDITS GREAT AND SMALL

Brendan Behan claimed: 'Critics are like eunuchs in a harem, they know how it's done, they've seen it done every day, but they're unable to do it themselves.' That may be true in the theatre but not so in sport. Pundits come in all shapes and styles. There's the George Hook school: 'Ireland are a bit like Pamela Anderson: when they're good they're great, when they're bad they're awful.' There's the unique Jason McAteer. When asked what positives

Giovanni Trapattoni would take from Ireland's 1–1 draw with the Czech Republic, Trigger replied: 'The major positive is this winning mentality.' Then there's the stating the bleeding obvious tradition personified by Greg Rusedski: 'In what other sport do you play six hours of tennis.' Then there is the special case of Ray Wilkins: 'Fàbregas literally carries ten yards of space around in his shorts.'

Pundits have to carefully negotiate the landmines along the way, like speaking too soon. Just after Niall Quinn, assuming that the 2011–12 League title was on its way to Old Trafford, stated: 'This is probably Alex Ferguson's greatest achievement.' Manchester City scored two late, late goals against QPR to claim the title.

Statistics are a limited weapon in the pundit's arsenal. David Letterman: 'Fifty per cent of the recent winners at Augusta have been left-handed.' Bubba Watson: 'Yeah, but fifty per cent are right-handed too.'

The best pundit's can spot the unusual. A classic of this kind was Sky Sports' Mark Robson's observation during Munster's Heineken Cup game away to Northampton, noting 'ROG' embossed on Ronan O'Gara's boots: 'That's just one letter short of God backwards.'

The GAA has pundits noted for their eloquence like Martin Carney's response to Donegal's second All-Ireland triumph: 'From their tip of Malin to the southerly point of the Drowes river; to the hills, the valleys and the towns along the majestic coastline; through the wild wilderness of the Bluestacks – this will be celebrated like no other.'

Then there is the tongue-in-cheek (or was it wishful thinking?), like Tomás Mulcahy after Brian Cody's achievement in leading Kilkenny to victory in the 2012 All-Ireland final replay over Galway: 'You'd be hoping now that maybe he would take time out, maybe to be cutting the lawn, or take up a bit of golf, or train the Kilkenny footballers for a change, or something like that. This is never-ending stuff.'

PARALYSIS BY ANALYSIS

From the outset, television pundits have a history of extending the boundaries of the English language. As a number of them have struggled to keep their brain and tongue in tune they have also spawned an explosion of 'Colemanballs'. The word 'Colemanballs' comes from David Coleman, a broadcaster whose name is synonymous with sporting howlers. The BBC commentator is remembered for a series of gaffes of which the following are but a tiny sample:

This man could be a dark horse.

The late start is due to the time.

He's thirty-one this year; last year he was thirty.

The pace of this match is really accelerating, by which I mean it is getting faster all the time.

One of the great unknown champions because very little is known about him.

Some names to look forward to – perhaps in the future.

Her time was four minutes thirteen seconds, which she is capable of.

This could be a repeat of what will happen at the European Games, next week.

This race is all about racing.

David Bedford is the athlete of all-time in the 1970s.

It doesn't mean anything, but what it does mean is that Abde Bile is very relaxed.

There is Brendan Foster, by himself, with 20,000 people.

John Aldridge on Sky Sports typifies this trend among soccer pundits: 'There's only one club in Europe you can leave Man United for – Real Madrid or Barcelona.'

Indeed a new word, 'Ron-glish', was invented for Ron Atkinson (before he lost his job as a pundit, or in pundit parlance 'took an early bath', following racist remarks about Chelsea's Marcel Desailly) because of the Do-Ron-Ron-Ron's unique use of the English language such as, 'I never comment on referees and I'm not going to break the habit of a lifetime for that prat' and 'I met Mick Jagger when I was playing for Oxford United and the Rolling Stones played a concert there. Little did I know that one day he'd be almost as famous as me.'

Those who watch football on ITV and BBC know that generally there's nothing being said. Most of our time we are subjected to questions and answers on ITV like:

Dickie Davis: 'What's he going to be telling his team at half-time, Denis?'
Denis Law: 'He'll be telling them that there are forty-five minutes left to play.'

The BBC equivalent is:

John Motson: 'Well, Trevor, what does this substitution mean tactically?'
Trevor Brooking: 'Well, Barnes, has come off and Rocastle has come on.'

Speed of Thought

Live television is like a trapeze act without a net below. Television pundits have to think on their feet. The late Maurice O'Doherty was one of the most famous people in Ireland when he read the main news on RTÉ television. He was very laid-back and came in to read the news at a minute to nine each night. One evening Maurice was finishing the news when he came to the weather. He looked at the page and it was blank. Maurice, being the true professional that he was, said: 'And the weather will continue for the next twenty-four hours.'

Not everybody, though, appreciates the current crop of GAA pundits. They tell a story about the adventures of *The Sunday Game* on the fairways. Colm O'Rourke and Kevin McStay, were out playing golf, and they decided to put some competition into the game by putting some serious money on the round – one euro. With such a sum at stake both of them were concentrating fiercely, and were perfectly matched for the first nine holes. On the tenth, though, McStay drove into the rough and couldn't find his ball. He called Colm over to help and the pair of them searched around. Finally, desperate to avoid the four-stroke penalty for a lost ball, McStay popped a new ball out of his pocket when Colm wasn't looking.

'Colm, I've found the ball,' McStay said.

'You filthy, cheating swine!' exploded Colm. 'I never thought that any friend of mine would stoop so low as to cheat in a game that had money on it.'

'I'm not cheating!' Kevin protested, 'I've found my ball, and I'll play it where it lies.'

'That's not your ball,' snarled Colm. 'I've been standing on your ball for the last five minutes.'

DANCING ON THE CEILING

Liam Griffin has probably produced one of the best soundbites in the history of GAA punditry: 'Hurling is the Riverdance of sport.' Some of Liam's musings though are more enigmatic: 'We need to look at more bottoms-up in hurling.'

GAA analysts are not to be taken too seriously. Hence, I enjoy the story of the traveller wandering on an island inhabited entirely by cannibals and coming upon a butcher's shop, which specialised in human brains. The human brains were differentiated by source. A sign in the shop read: 'Scientists' brains £20 a lb: economists' brains £40 a lb: philosophers' brains £60 a lb and GAA analysts' brains £2000 a lb.'

The traveller asked how was it that GAA analysts' brains were so expensive. The butcher said: 'Its because you have to kill a hundred times more GAA analysts to get a pound of brains.'

AH REF!

The most common criticism by GAA officialdom about *The Sunday Game* is about its use of video evidence in what it calls 'trial by television'. The GAA could learn from the way other sports use video evidence. In 2000 twenty-two-year-old Tracy Sargent streaked at an indoor bowls event. One could not but be impressed by the diligence of the officials and their commitment to the cause of duty. They later issued a statement: 'Having studied the incident on forty-three occasions, including slow-motion replays, we have decided against implementing a rule that spectators should remain clothed at all times.'

Mind you, there are also pitfalls to be avoided when it comes to video evidence. Many years ago when Jimmy Hill was the chairman of Fulham, his club were due to face an FA inquiry after some of their players were involved in a brawl after a match with Gillingham. Hill set out to prove that Fulham should not be held responsible with a video presentation of the game's flashpoints.

He was very pleased with his efforts and boasted to friends before the inquiry that the FA should be selling tickets for his presentation. However, when he produced his video as evidence he was shocked to discover that his wife had taped a cookery programme over it!

FORGIVE US OUR TRESPASSES

Admhaím do Dhia uilechumhachtach
agus daoibshe, a bhráithre,
gur pheacaigh mé go trom.
A Thiarna, déan trócaire.

If you didn't understand those last four lines you have no chance of ever raising to even lowly office in the GAA. Those of you who did will recognise it as a prayer asking for forgiveness and mercy. Sadly, given their propensity to put their feet in their mouths this is the prayer GAA pundits have to say the most often!

PRISON BREAK

A journalist with the *Roscommon Herald* was writing a feature about prison life in Mountjoy Prison and was interviewing one of the prisoners: 'Do you watch much television here?'

'Only *The Sunday Game's* football analysis,' the inmate said.

'That's too bad,' the reporter said, 'But I do think its nice the governor lets you watch that.'

'It's not nice,' replied the prisoner. 'It's the toughest part of our punishment.'

KISS YOUR ASS

Into every pundit's life some rain must fall. Fans are keenly aware of the moral of the GAA analyst, the donkey and the bridge. A man and his son were bringing their donkey to the fair. The man was walking with the donkey and his son was up on the animal's back. A passer-by said: 'Isn't it a disgrace to see that poor man walking and the young fellow up on the donkey having an easy time. He should walk and let his poor father have a rest.'

So the boy dismounted and the father took his place. A mile later they met another man who said: 'Isn't it a disgrace to have that boy walking while his father takes it easy. You should both get up on the donkey's back.'

They duly did but a short time later they met an enraged woman who screamed: 'How cruel it is to have two healthy men up on that poor donkey's back. The two of you should get down and carry the donkey.' Again they did as they were told but the donkey fell into the river as they walked over the bridge and drowned.

The moral is that if you are an analyst and you are trying to please everyone you might as well kiss your ass goodbye.

THOSE MAGNIFICENT MEN IN THEIR FLYING MACHINES

A man is flying in a hot air balloon and realises he is lost. He reduces height and spots a man down below. He lowers the balloon further and shouts: 'Excuse me, can you tell me where I am?'

Kevin McStay below says: 'Yes, you're in a hot-air balloon, hovering thirty feet above this field.'

'You must be a GAA pundit,' says the balloonist.

'I am,' replies McStay. 'How did you know?'

'Well,' says the balloonist, 'everything you have told me is technically correct, but it's no use to anyone.'

McStay says, 'You must be a GAA referee.'

'I am,' replies the balloonist, 'But how did you know?'

'Well,' says McStay, 'you don't know where you are, or where you're going and you're in the same position you were before we met, but now it's my fault.'

A PUNDIT'S DICTIONARY

Q. How many pundits does it take to change a light bulb?

A. None. They just sit there in the dark and complain.

BULLISH

Most pundit-speak induces a state of Deja Moo: the feeling that you've heard this bull before. The following is a reminder of what words actually mean in pundit-speak:

I'm sorry: You'll be sorry.

We need: I want.

It's the manager's decision: My correct decision should be obvious by now.

Do what you want: You'll pay for this later.

We need to talk: I need to complain.

Sure go ahead: I don't want you to.

I'm not upset: Of course I'm upset.

DOCTOR'S ORDERS

Five surgeons are discussing who makes the best patients for them to operate on. The first surgeon says, 'Accountants are the best to operate on because when you open them up, everything inside is numbered.'

The second responds, 'Try electricians. Everything inside them is colour-coded.'

The third surgeon says, 'No, librarians are the best. Everything inside them is in alphabetical order.'

The fourth surgeon intercedes, 'I like construction workers … they always understand when you have a few parts left over at the end and when it takes longer than you expect.'

To which the fifth surgeon says: 'You're all wrong. GAA pundits are the easiest. There's no guts, no heart, no spine and their heads and butts are intertwined.'

BONFIRE OF THE VANITIES

Many GAA stars' attitude to journalism is summed up in the story of God and the devil: On the first day God created the sun, the devil countered and created sunburn. On the second day God created sex, the devil created – marriage. On the third day God created a journalist. The devil deliberated throughout the fourth day and on the fifth day the devil created – another journalist.

A MODERN-DAY MIRACLE

It is a little-known fact but some football fans think of Cyril Farrell as a lifesaver and a miracle-worker. One Cork supporter was in a horrific car crash. He was on a life-support machine for several weeks. All kinds of prayers were said and holy medals were placed on his forehead but to no avail. As he was a mad hurling fan someone, in a fit of desperation, brought in a VCR beside his bed and stuck on a video of Cyril's highlights. As soon as he made his first comments the comatose patient got up from his bed and switched off the video. As astonished doctors and nurses looked on he said: 'That f**king idiot was wrecking my head.'

TESTING TIMES

The RTÉ Sports Department decided that it should have a test for all its sport pundits. After the exam the supervisor pulled Pat Spillane over to his desk and said, 'Pat, I have a feeling that you have been cheating on your tests.'

'What makes you think that?' Spillane asked him.

'Well,' said the supervisor, 'I was looking over your test. The first question was "Who is the leader of the Conservative Party?"

Colm O'Rourke, who sat next to you, put David Cameron and so did you.'

'Everyone knows that he is the leader of the Tories,' Spillane defended himself.

'Well, the next question was "Who was the Conservative leader before David Cameron?" O'Rourke put "I don't know" and you put "Me neither".'

NAVAN MAN

By profession, Colm O'Rourke is a teacher in St Patrick's, Navan but there is no question in the eyes of many that he is the most authoritative pundit on gaelic football. Although he is best known for his incisive analysis he has supplied many a good quote down through the years. A baker's dozen, in order of no importance, of O'Rourkisms:

1. Dublin were the 'nearly team' in 2002 but as any farmer will tell you nearly never bulled a cow.

2. Joe Brolly always talked a great game. The problem was that he didn't always play a great one!
   O'Rourke responding to a Joe Brolly after dinner speech which had a few digs at the Meath team O'Rourke starred on.

3. If Adam was an Armagh footballer, Eve would have no chance. Instead of an apple, he would have looked for a banana, as this is on the diet sheet.

4. Benny Coulter has a left foot in the right place.

5. It's a play-the-man-forget-about-the-ball type of game.

6. Who doses the bullocks in the country any more? The poor auld farmers. Every team needs a couple of farmers.

7. When your luck is out your bullocks don't fatten.

8. If a fella was driving a load of straw through the Down defence the Down backs still wouldn't be able to get their hands to it.

9. Down's plan last year was to kick the ball to Benny Coulter, and if that didn't work to kick it even more to Benny Coulter.

10. Mothers kept a Mick Lyons photo on the mantlepiece to stop their children going too near the fire.

11. Ulster football is much more physical and that's before anyone breaks the rules.

12. The worst thing about the game was there wasn't even a chance of a row.

13. If you can't take a hard tackle, you should play table tennis.
    O'Rourke countering the charges that his Meath team were too physical.

BERNARD'S CHOICE

People think the life of a pundit in RTÉ is all about glamour. Not so. When you appear on a high-profile programme on national television you are not nearly as pampered as people expect. When Bernard Flynn went to the RTÉ canteen for his evening meal on his first day as a guest on *The Sunday Game* he asked, 'What are my choices?'

The man behind the counter replied, 'Yes or no.'

FAIR FIGHT

It is good when pundits have a bit of an edge to their comments. I would not be the biggest fan in the world of the BBC soccer coverage but I did enjoy, during the 2002 World Cup, Martin O'Neill's comment to Gary Lineker: 'You know what I like about you, Gary? Very little.'

Joe Brolly and Pat Spillane can have a testy relationship. Brolly describes how one night he was walking out of the RTÉ studios and he saw Spillane and one of his friends were being assaulted by a group of Kildare fans after Spillane had made yet another incendiary attack on the Lilywhites. Spillane yelled out: 'Joe could you give me and my friend some help.'

Brolly coolly replied: 'I'm always glad to help. You don't say: "Me and my friend." You say: "My friend and I." Then he got into his car and drove off.

A GRAVE MATTER

A bus load of GAA pundits were driving down a country road when all of a sudden, the bus ran off the road and crashed into a tree in the old farmer's field. The old farmer, after seeing what happened, went over to investigate. He then proceeded to dig a hole and bury the pundits.

A few days later, the local sergeant saw the crashed bus and asked the farmer where all the pundits had gone. The old farmer said he had buried them. The officer then asked the old farmer, 'Were they all dead?' The old farmer replied, 'Well, some of them said they weren't, but you know them pundits lie.'

SCHOOL REUNION

Des Cahill went to visit his old school. He asked the students if anyone could give him an example of a 'tragedy'. One boy stood up and offered the suggestion that, 'If my best friend who lives next door was playing in the street and a car came along and killed him, that would be a tragedy.'

'No,' Des said, 'that would be an *accident*.'

Another boy raised his hand. 'If a school bus carrying fifty children drove off a cliff, killing everybody involved, that would be a tragedy.'

'I'm afraid not,' explained Des, 'that is what we would call a *great loss.*' The room was silent; none of the other children volunteered. 'What?' asked Des. 'Is there no one here who can give me an example of a tragedy?'

Finally, a boy in the back raised his hand. In a timid voice, he spoke: 'If an aeroplane carrying you and *The Sunday Game* team were blown up by a bomb that would be a tragedy.'

'Wonderful.' Des beamed. 'Marvellous. And can you tell me why that would be a tragedy?'

'Well,' said the boy, 'because it wouldn't be an accident, and it certainly would be no great loss.'

On the Air

RTÉ licence-payers fork out significant sums each year to be entertained. RTÉ's gaelic games coverage takes this mandate seriously as the following compilation reveals:

They've lost nothing today – except pride and, of course, the Connacht title.

Marty Morrissey.

There won't be a cow milked in Clare tonight.
Marty Morrissey after Clare won the 1992 Munster final.

Lovely piece of wholehearted fielding. Mick O'Connell stretched like Nureyev for a one-handed catch.

Micheál O'Hehir.

And here comes Nudie Hughes for Nudie reason.

Micheál O'Hehir.

Remember, postcards only, please. The winner will be the first one opened.

Liam Campbell.

The Ulster championship makes the Colosseum look like a bouncy castle at a kid's party.

Tony Davis.

If you didn't know him, you wouldn't know who he was.
Celebrity Jigs and Reels star Paul Curran.

An easy kick for Peter Canavan but, as everybody knows, no kicks are easy.

Martin Carney.

Identify the Derry captain: Anthony Hopkins, Anthony Clare or Anthony Tohill.

Sunday Game competition.

He grabs the sliotar, he's on the fifty … he's on the forty … he's on the thirty … he's on the ground.

Micheál Ó Muircheartaigh.

SH*T-FACED

An elderly farmer in a remote part of Leitrim finally decided to buy a television. The shopkeeper assured him that this would install the antenna and TV the next day. The next evening the farmer turned on his new TV and found only the pundits on *The Sunday Game* on every channel. The next morning he turned the TV on and found only *The Sunday Game* no matter what channel he put on. The next day the same again so he called the shop to complain. The owner said it was impossible for every channel to only have the GAA pundits talking, but agreed to send the repairman to check the TV. When the TV repairman turned on the TV he was stunned to find the farmer was right. After looking at the TV for a while he went outside to check the antenna. In a few minutes he returned and told the farmer he had found the problem. The antenna had been installed on top of the windmill and grounded to the manure spreader.

The repairman sagely remarked: 'GAA pundits are like nappies. They need to be changed often and for the same reason.'

MAN OF THE YEAR

Despite challenges from Marty Morrissey – and Marty's elevation to sex symbol status – 2013 was the year of Joe Brolly. Nobody watching will ever forget his comment after *that* tackle on Monaghan's Conor McManus: 'He's a brilliant footballer but you can forget about Seán Cavanagh as a man.' Brolly's celebrated rant made him the unquestioned Pundit of the Year in 2013.

In fairness, the competition was not of a very high standard. There was the bizarre, in the form of Dion Dublin: 'Sandro's holding his face. You can tell from that it's a knee injury.'

There was the stating-the-bleeding-obvious in Ray Wilkins: 'Frank Lampard has still got the game legs he had five years ago.'

There was the least insightful in the form of Paul Merson: 'I think Southampton will finish above teams that are well below them.' Merson confirmed his place in this category with: 'If you don't give Martinez a chance, what chance has he got?'

Of course there was the ever-popular literal in Tony Cascarino: 'David Moyes was just staring at me with his eyes. Literally.' Dion Dublin also got in on the act with: 'Aston Villa literally meta-phorically had their pants pulled down.'

As is to be expected, there was the baffling in the unique take of Kevin Keegan: 'Manchester City are built on sand – and I don't mean that because their owners are from the Arab countries.'

Jamie Redknapp continued to occupy a distinctive place in the world of punditry with comments such as: 'We have a number of two-footed players in this country at the moment – Morrison, Barkley, Townsend – and they are unique.'

Billy Dodds tops the can-you-believe-he-just-said-that category with: 'We've given the lad some stick for diving, but these days he's come on leaps and bounds.'

Robbie Savage won the mixed metaphor category with: 'You need to take your rose-scented glasses off, mate.'

Tony Mowbray made the prediction of the year: 'Instant success is what everybody wants. Fortunately I've got an owner who's patient.' Three weeks later he was sacked by Middlesbrough.

Closer to home, Eamonn Dunphy was not holding back on the subject of Noel King: 'He makes Trapattoni seem like Pep Guardiola.'

Roy Keane made an unexpected bid for the title of comedian of year with his observation: 'You obviously don't know Martin [O'Neill] as well as you think you do – he makes me look like Mother Teresa.'

Jim Gavin, at the post All-Ireland final press conference, was the clear winner in the poor mouth award: 'The minute the referee blows the final whistle, that's when the 2013 season ends. I know from speaking to other managers, they're already setting themselves up for the 2014 championship. We're probably behind now already.'

Eamonn O'Hara did make a challenge for Brolly's crown with his devastating critique of Kevin Walsh after Sligo's defeat to London in the Connacht championship and even more so because of the exuberance of his suits on *The Sunday Game*.

Pat Spillane was another contender with: 'Jamie Clarke is the Messi of Ulster football.'

However, no one could touch Joe, especially with gems such as his dismissal of Pat Spillane's analysis of the Dublin versus Cork quarter-final in 2013 as a chess match: 'It is, only you wouldn't see Kasparov taking Karpov and dragging him across the table and down to the turf as he was about to check-mate him.'

There was also: 'Sweet mother of all the Brollys.' Joe's reaction to the suggestion that Galway might have beaten Mayo in the 2013 Connacht championship.

Brolly also provided the analogy of the year: 'The GAA is powerful. It's like the Masons without the handshakes.'

BROTHERS IN ARMS

Joe Brolly did not have it all his own way though. Armagh manager Paul Grimley swiped back at Brolly's criticism after Armagh's defeat to Cavan in 2013: 'One thing my brothers didn't do was go around Croke Park or any other park blowing kisses to the crowd.'

SKY HIGH

On April Fool's Day the GAA announced a seismic shift with their deal with Sky television for exclusive rights to some of their championship games. *Liveline* went into meltdown with irate fans. It was as if the sky had fallen in. Happily there were many light comments that poked fun at the deal including: 'Let's look forward to Sky Sports Super Sliotar Saturday.'

It can be exclusively revealed in these pages that Sky are about to take on RTÉ in a bidding war for the rights to another bastion of Irish television, the Angelus.

EVERY GIRL'S CRAZY ABOUT A SHARP DRESSED MAN

Predictably, Sky's first live GAA match, Kilkenny's demolition of Offaly, created a lot of interest on social media. In Ireland most of the comment was about the magnificence of Jamesie O'Connor's new suit but in England the tone of the comments was a unique mixture of amusement and bemusement. One viewer tweeted: 'Just watched 5 mins of hurling, WTF is going on there's a GK but they keep smashing it over the bar how the f**k does he save that?'

Another remarked: 'Hurling on Sky! Brilliant idea. Superb … skill and violence.'

One observed: 'Watching this Irish Hurling on Sky Sports confirms my belief that the Irish are mental.'

Mental well-being was again the concern of another viewer: 'Looks like it takes a lot of nerve, balls and I suspect some insanity to want to be a goalie in this.'

I'VE GOT FRIENDS IN LOW PLACES
Garth Brooks announced with great fanfare that he would make his comeback in Croke Park. One fan remarked: 'He must be from Mayo. He'll play Croke Park five times and still get no medal.'

IF TOMORROW NEVER COMES
In July 2014 Croke Park was once again the focal point for a raging national debate. This time though it was about the debacle over the Garth Brooks concert. A new acronym was suggested for the GAA's CCCC: The Central Concerts Cock-ups Committee.

IT DOESN'T ADD UP
Some cynics were very unsympathetic to the huge loss of revenue for the GAA with the news of the cancellation of the concerts – on the basis that they had agreed to three concerts a year but then went for eight. Hence the new name, the NGAA: The Not Great Arithmetic Association.

CHAPTER FIFTEEN

Nice Things Tyrone Fans Say About Pat Spillane

This chapter has been left blank to reflect accurately the level of affection felt for Pat in Tyrone since his 'puke football' comments.

Mind you, after his infamous 'rant' about Tyrone, and Seán Cavanagh in particular, their fans may now be feeling the same way about Joe Brolly.

Chapter Sixteen

Come on the Rossies

The GAA needs characters. Roscommon's former goalkeeper Shane 'Cake' Curran is certainly one of them.

In 2012 *Bridesmaids* star and former minor Roscommon goalkeeper Chris O'Dowd said on *The Sunday Game* that his hero was Shane Curran. His description of Curran was seen as spot on: 'He's likely to ride a bull into a church.'

Curran first exploded on to the national consciousness in the 1989 Connacht minor football final. Roscommon trailed Galway by two points when they were awarded a penalty in the last minute. Peadar Glennon, corner-forward with the Rossies, placed the ball on the spot and steeped to take the kick. Out of the blue Shane raced forward and blasted the ball past the Galway goalie. There was chaos. Roscommon were presented with the cup but subsequently had the game taken away in the smoky GAA corridors of power. Eventually the Rossies won the replay ordered by the Connacht Council.

The Road Not Taken

Few people get the last word with Sir Alex Ferguson but legend has it that in his soccer days Shane Curran was a rare exception. Whilst on trial with Manchester United, and uncertain about his future, Shane asked Fergie directly: 'What's going on?'

As Sir Alex was being evasive Shane interrupted in him in full flow and said: 'Alex, it's like this. If you can't handle Paul McGrath you certainly can't handle me.' Curran immediately walked away from his career with United.

A CROWD FAVOURITE

A lot of people still remember the way Curran whipped up the Roscommon crowd into a frenzy with his antics in Croke Park against Kerry in the All-Ireland quarter-final in 2003, not to mention the way he scored a goal and an incredible point from the goalkeeper's position against Sligo in the Connacht championship in 2004. What people may forget is that way back in 1992 he played in the Roscommon full-forward line in the Connacht championship against Leitrim. Mind you he was just as animated back then when the Roscommon management substituted him!

Someone once asked him: 'So what's a forward doing playing in goal for Roscommon?'

Curran replied: 'I'm trying to keep the ball out.'

MISTAKEN IDENTITY

At the height of his career, Curran was in a well-known nightclub when he fell into conversation with a complete stranger. The combination of the loud music and the effects of a few glasses of something stronger than lemonade meant that the communication levels were not as they might have been. As they shook hands before parting Curran received an unusual request: 'Any chance if I give you my address you'd sign one of your CDs and send it on to me.'

A puzzled Curran inquired: 'Who exactly do you think I am?'

'You're the lad from the Saw Doctors, aren't you?'

Quick Thinking

In 2000 Shane won a Junior All-Ireland final with Roscommon. His manager Gay Sheeran has a vivid memory of the win:

> You never knew what would happen next with Shane. In the replay Kerry got a score and the Kerry lads were catching a breather. The referee turned his back and started running up the field when suddenly the ball went over his head and landed seventy yards up the pitch before Kerry knew what had happened. Karol Mannion was the only one alive to the situation and set up a point. We won that All-Ireland by a point. What the referee never realised was that Shane had kicked the ball out from his hands and that's why he got the ball up the field so quickly! That's typical of Shane. He could give you acute blood pressure at times but when his moments of madness came off he could be a match winner.

Frankie Says

Curran's teammate with both Roscommon and St Brigid's is Frankie Dolan. Like his brother Garvin, Frankie had a turbulent relationship with referees and umpires. When Frankie got married at Christmas 2010 some of the guests were surprised to see so many referees invited. One referee was told in no uncertain terms: 'You were lucky to get an invite.' The official coolly replied: 'I know, especially as I booked Garvin for the way he walked out of the church.'

The father of the bride had been a GAA umpire and brought the house down at the speeches during the reception when he recalled his first encounter with Frankie, when he was umpiring a match and Dolan had sent a shot inches wide. After signalling the ball wide his future son-in-law raced in to tell him in the most emphatic terms that he was a 'f**king boll*x'. Just as he was regaining his composure he was accosted from behind by Dolan's father, Frankie senior, who also told him that he was a 'f**king boll*x'.

Not to be outdone, the best man also had a big hit with the crowd when in his speech he said: 'Frankie has brought unique distinction to his club, his county and his province whenever he represented them' – dramatic pause – 'in a bar or nightclub.'

FRANKIE GOES TO HOLLYWOOD

In the Connacht final in 2001 Roscommon's Frankie Dolan was perceived by some Mayo fans as engaging in 'theatricals' which 'caused' a Mayo player to be sent off. They gave him a new nickname 'Frankie goes to Hollywood'.

WEIGHTY MATTERS

Frankie's waistline may no longer be of inter-county requirements but playing for St Brigid's he can still do what most forwards can't do and that's score points. After Frankie starred for Brigid's in their third consecutive Connacht club title in 2012 Pat Spillane was moved to write: 'The GAA needs more Frankie Dolans and less [champion runner] Freddie Fredericks.'

THE BARE ESSENTIALS

It seems to be forgotten by most people that Tommy Carr began his career as a footballer with Tipperary. It is something he does not always like to be reminded of! In a way he is quite similar in character to his friend John Maughan because fitness and discipline were the hallmarks of their managerial style. The fact that both have an army background may have something to do with it.

Carr brought new discipline to the Rossies when he became their manager. It was badly needed. Two Roscommon players' talent for playing pool in the nude made headlines in 2002. When a second major breach of discipline occurred that summer the Roscommon County Board decided to disband the entire county panel. Given the penchant for nude pool among his senior county players Tom Mullaney, then Secretary of the Roscommon County Board, showed a flair for double entendre in his appraisal of the disciplinary measures, 'As a group, all players hang together or hang separately.'

Writing in the *Irish Times*, Keith Duggan's verdict on that Roscommon policy of 'total disclosure' when playing pool made for amusing reading, 'Ah yes, the career of the gaelic footballer can end in a flash. Just ask any of the Roscommon senior players. It will take many, many years before a Roscommon senior manager can stand before his team in the dressing room and bellow the traditional GAA rallying cry, "Show them yez have the balls for it lads."'

In 2011 when Fergal O'Donnell stepped down as Roscommon County Manager Joe Brolly referred back to the county's former indignities: 'Fergal O'Donnell's resignation as County Manager left the people of Roscommon in shock. The big man did an excellent job. When he began his tenure, Roscommon were a laughing stock – some of their past antics made the English rugby team's dwarf-throwing look like a quiet night in over a hot cup of cocoa.'

SHINE ON

In 1975 the most famous piece of music journalism was written. A reviewer went to a concert given by a guy nobody ever heard of and wrote: 'I've seen the future of rock and roll and his name is Bruce Springsteen.' In 2006, having seen a new star tear into the opposition with the same relish that Tiny Tim tucked into the family's Christmas ham, I sent a text to Dermot Earley which stated: 'I've seen the future of Roscommon football and his name is Donie Shine.'

Like Earley before him, Shine wears his fame slightly and both became ambassadors for Roscommon as much for their characters off the pitch as their brilliance on it. The difference is that Donie has a much higher female fan base than Dermot ever had.

According to rumour Take That wrote their number one song 'Let it Shine' about him. I've been unable to confirm the veracity of the story with Gary Barlow.

If there's ever a DVD made of the history of Roscommon his winning point in the 2010 Connacht final will be one of the iconic moments.

Donie has seen his share of uncomfortable moments in the county jersey:

In the 2006 All-Ireland minor final we were playing Kerry when our goalie Mark Miley made a rare error which cost us a point. The game ended in a draw and as I walked into the tunnel I could see Mark was disconsolate but I wasn't sure what to say to him. When I got into the dressing room Mark was there with his head in his hands. Everybody felt very awkward. Then Conor Devanney came in and said immediately: 'Mark, for Jaysus sake, what the hell were you at?' Everybody laughed. It broke the tension and we all moved on. It seemed the worst possible thing he could have said but actually it was the best possible thing. Of course in the replay Mark went on to keep his record of not conceding a goal in the championship intact.

In the Name of the Father

Donie is called after his father, who both played for and managed Roscommon. Donie Snr has witnessed some unusual motivational speeches:

A club team from Roscommon travelled two hundred miles to a tournament game in Cork. At half-time they trailed by 7–2 to 0–5. A crisis meeting was held in the middle of the pitch. Recriminations were flying until the captain called for silence and an end to the bickering and a hush descended. One player said, 'We need some positive encouragement.'

After a short delay the manager-cum-trainer-cum-club secretary-cum-groundskeeper said, 'Come on now lads. Let's go out there and show them up. It's plain to be seen. They can't score points!'

EARLEY TO RISE

Former Roscommon star Paul Earley is a regular analyst on Setanta television. However, in a previous incarnation he was a regular presence on *The Sunday Game*. One of his best moments came after the 1988 All-Ireland semi-final when Mayo, managed by John O'Mahony, put up a credible showing before losing to mighty Meath. At the end Michael Lyster asked Earley: 'Will Mayo be back?' Quick as a flash Paul replied: 'I hope not!'

SIMPLY THE BEST

When Robert Kennedy was assassinated in 1968 his brother Ted said at the funeral that he 'need not be enlarged in death beyond what he was in life but to be remembered simply as a good and decent man who saw wrong and tried to right it, saw suffering and tried to heal it'. The life of the dead is placed in the memories of the living. The love we feel in life keeps people alive beyond their time. Anyone who has given love will always live on in another's heart. The stars in the sky are not the eyes of God but the stars of those who have passed on lovingly watching over us. Dermot Earley's star will shine the brightest.

Earley was one of the greatest players never to win an All-Ireland medal. The closest he came to it was the controversial 1980 All-Ireland final when Roscommon lost to Kerry. The Roscommon fans were irate about the refereeing of the game. Legend has it that one of them approached the referee immediately after the game and said, 'Hi ref, how's your dog?'

The ref is said to have replied, 'What do you mean? I don't have a dog.'

The fan responded, 'That's strange. You're the first blind man I've ever met that doesn't have a guide dog!'

THUD

Another time Roscommon were paying Galway in the Connacht championship when Earley was tearing through the defence and heading for goal. Peter Lee came across and body-checked him, stopping him. Micheál Ó Muircheartaigh was commentating on the match. He described the incident, 'Dermot Earley is thundering through. He's stopped by Peter Lee. He's [Peter] not a big man.' Then there was a pause, 'But he is a broad man.' Earley was left on the seat of his pants.

SEX IN THE CITY

Dermot was always incredibly focused in his preparations, not just for games but also for training sessions. One of the messers on the team, who must remain nameless, decided to throw him a curveball one day and asked him if he would have sex before a match, expecting an indignant reaction. Dermot decided to turn defence into attack and calmly said: 'Well I might but not if it was a big match. How about yourself?' The player in question went as red as beetroot and for the first time in history was speechless.

That is Seamus Hayden's version of the story. Dermot's own account is that Gerry Emmett asked him once if he would have sex before a match and he replied: 'No. It would slow me down too much.'

Gerry cautiously inquired: 'How much would it slow you down by?'

Dermot's response was instantaneous: 'One tenth of a second.'

EXCUSE ME

After he retired from football, Earley managed the Roscommon team for two years. During his stewardship, a fringe member of the squad missed a number of training sessions. Earley tried to make contact with him but with no success. He had to resort to leaving him messages in all kinds of strange locations. A few days later he got a message on his answering machine, 'Dermot this is X. I'm sorry I missed the last four training sessions. My reasons were compelling and undescribable.' So ended the message and his brief and undistinguished career as a Roscommon footballer.

LAST ORDERS

Dermot was an ardent disciple of the school of positive thinking. One of his favourite stories to stress the message of 'having a go' was about Brendan Behan. The great writer was being interviewed on Canadian television and was clearly under the influence. The irate interviewer asked him bluntly how he could have the temerity to be drunk on live television. Behan replied: 'I was sitting in a pub in Dublin last week and I saw a beer mat which said: "Drink Canada dry." So when I got here I said I would give it a go.'

Déjà Vu

Dermot was a brilliant speaker and invariably told a joke against himself in each speech. One night he was approaching Roscommon town when he saw a teenager thumbing a lift. As it was raining he picked him up. As they got close to the football pitch Dermot asked the youngster if he had ever played in Dr Hyde Park. The young man replied: 'Many times.'

Dermot said: 'I played a few good games here myself. In 1973 Roscommon were playing the All-Ireland champions of the time, Cork, here. The team were just a point ahead in the last minute when Cork mounted an attack and I made the saving clearance.'

The teenager replied: 'I know.'

Dermot continued: 'In 1977 I played on with a broken finger and helped Roscommon beat Galway in the Connacht final.'

Again the young man responded: 'I know.'

Undeterred Dermot persisted: 'I once kicked a forty-five against a gale force wind and landed it over the bar in a match against Down.'

Yet again the young man's reply was: 'I know.'

By now Dermot was puzzled and asked his companion what age he was. When his guest replied that he was only sixteen Dermot asked: 'All those matches were over twenty years ago, before you were even born. How could you possibly know about them?'

The teenager sighed deeply before saying: 'You gave me a lift two weeks ago and you told me the exact same things then.'

Supermac

Another star of the Roscommon team that Earley played on was Tony McManus, not just because of his skill but because of the intelligent way he played the game. A revealing insight into the sharpness of Tony's mind came in a county final between his club Clann na nGael and Kilmore. At one point a Clann player grabbed the ball. One of his opponents called him by the christian name. Instinctively the Clann player passed the ball to him and the Kilmore player raced up the field. Shortly after Tony McManus won possession and the same Kilmore man yelled, 'Tony, Tony, pass the ball.' Tony swung around and said, 'If I was playing with you, I wouldn't pass you the ball!'

The View from Washington

Gay Sheeran played with Tony McManus before going on to manage the Rossies in the 1990s. He had a number of memorable moments in his career:

> I know it seems heresy to many people but the bond I felt and still feel for the players on the county team is much stronger than I do for the lads in the club. The reason for it is very simple, I spent so much time with them. When I was managing I quickly found out that I was a lot older than I thought. We were playing a match on a wet day and Dermot Washington was wearing only one glove. The conversation unfolded as follows:
>
> Me: 'You're like Jimmy Mannion. He would always wear only one glove.'
> Dermot: 'Who's Jimmy Mannion?'
> Me: 'How can you not know Jimmy Mannion? He was on the Roscommon team that won the Connacht final in 1972 and got to the League final in 1974.'
> Dermot: 'I wasn't even born in 1974.'

Famous Seamus

Seamus Hayden was a Roscommon midfielder in the 1980 All-Ireland final. He was in charge of a club team and they had a very high age profile. One night Seamus rang one of the officials in St

Dominics club who was in the middle of a crisis meeting. The club had been going through some difficulties and could not get anybody to manage them. The meeting was going badly and they were getting nowhere so eventually the great Jimmy Murray, who was eighty-two years of age at the time, said he would train the team until they could get someone else to take over. At that moment Seamus's call came through and when the official answered he said: 'Hayden, you ugly hoor how's it going?'

Seamus politely let this insult pass and inquired about what was going on in the club. The official replied: 'Well it's like this. Jimmy Murray has a dilemma. He's not sure whether at that this stage of his life he should train Dominics or play for your team!'

ON THE BENCH

Danny Murray is the only Roscommon player to win All-Star awards in consecutive years, in 1979 and 1980. He was famous in the squad for his propensity to have a steak for lunch before a big game. Danny's happiest memories are of the players on the team:

> Probably the great character in the squad was Gerry Emmett. It seemed Gerry was the perpetual sub but it never got him down. The Connacht Council had a special celebration for us to mark the anniversary of one of our Connacht titles in McHale Park in Castlebar at half-time. Before the first half finished there was an announcement over the loudspeaker: 'Would the 1980 Roscommon team please go to the dugout.' One of the lads asked: 'Where's the dugout?' Quick as a flash Gerry interjected: 'I'll show ye. I know every dugout in every county in Ireland.'

NO PAT ON THE BACK

Pat Lindsay was Roscommon's greatest full-back. In 1979 he captained Roscommon to its first and only National League title, with a crushing defeat of a star-laden Cork team. His Roscommon

242

colleagues would not allow him to get too big for his boots though: 'Eamon McManus said to me: "If you ever get up the midfield area, that's for skillful players, pass the ball to someone with a bit of skill."'

No Dirty Harry

Throughout Lindsay's career he stood right beside Harry Keegan, who is the only Roscommon player to have won three All-Star awards. Harry has seen some bizarre sights in his career:

> I will never forget the 1972 All-Ireland semi-final against Kerry. The game is probably most remembered for the long time Mick O'Connell sat down in the middle of the pitch tying his laces. To some people in Roscommon it was a bit disrespectful.

However, it is a trip to America that stands out for him:

> Long before Cork made striking fashionable in the GAA we were the first to threaten to use player power. We were in New York to play Kerry in the Cardinal Cushing Games over two matches. We beat them initially in a thirteen-a-side in the first game. We had been promised money from John Kerry O'Donnell, who was 'Mr GAA' in New York. We knew for a fact that Kerry had been paid but we got nothing and we were running short of money. A council of war was held by the Roscommon players, appropriately under Dermot Earley. The word was sent back to John Kerry – no money no playing. As far as I know we were the first county to threaten to strike!
>
> Another memory I have of the trip is that we were invited to a formal reception hosted by the Lord Mayor. It was a real big deal for the County Board. The problem was that the heat was almost unbearable. One of the lads brought down a keg of beer to keep himself distracted from the heat! The late Gerry Beirne went so far as to take off his shirt, which was a major breach of protocol. The message quickly came down from the top table

from the County Chairman, Michael O'Callaghan, to get it back on quickly.

The American influence was soon felt in an unexpected way in Roscommon when team coach Seán Young asked the players to kneel down and say a prayer before running out on to the pitch.

MANAGING THE MONEY

Keegan is very appreciative of the role played by the Roscommon County Board, though their methods were unorthodox:

> They always looked after us even if the money wasn't too generous. One incident stands out for me. After a Connacht final in the 1970s I went to one of the top officials in the County Board and told him that I needed money for expenses. He brought me out to his car, opened the boot and pulled out a £100 note from a green Wellington and handed it to me. He then told me to send in the docket for it.

AN AWKWARD MOMENT

A generation before Tony McManus and Dermot Earley the star of the Roscommon team was Gerry O'Malley. Gerry was also a wonderful hurler. At one stage he played for Connacht against Munster in a Railway Cup match. At the time the balance of power in hurling was heavily weighted towards Munster but Connacht ran them close enough. On the way home Gerry stopped off in Clare for a drink with the legendary Galway hurler, Inky Flaherty. Given the interest in hurling in the Banner County the barman recognised Inky straight away and said, 'Ye did very well.'

'Not too bad,' replied Inky.

'I suppose if it wasn't for O'Malley you would have won,' speculated the barman.

Flaherty answered back, 'Here he is beside me. Ask him yourself.'

A HOSPITAL PASS

In 1962 O'Malley played in his only All-Ireland football final when the Westerners lost heavily to Kerry. Gerry was injured and had to be taken to hospital after the match. He was in a bed beside a man he had never met before. His neighbour knew who Gerry was and they got to talking. The next day a man came in with the newspapers who didn't recognise Gerry from Adam and his new friend asked him, 'How did the papers say O'Malley played?'

'Brutal,' came the instant reply and it certainly left Gerry feeling even more brutal.

RADIO DAZE

Even if supporters of county teams are sometimes united by a general loathing of their neighbour, fans are the lifeblood of the GAA. In 1962 Roscommon's best-known fan Paddy Joe Burke was listening to his first ever All-Ireland semi-final in the family kitchen with half their neighbours in attendance, as was the norm in rural Ireland. His beloved Roscommon were trailing Cavan. Disaster struck when the batteries died temporarily and the commentary was lost. Paddy Joe's mother intervened immediately and told everyone to get on their knees and say the rosary. Such was the power of the their prayers that when the rosary was finished not alone was the radio working but Roscommon had taken lead and went on to win the match.

HEADY DAYS

Down through the years the GAA has produced a number of players who have had 'bad hair days'. A case in point would be the celebrated 'Rasher' Duignan of the great Clann na nGael club in Roscommon. As his career progressed his hairline receded, necessitating the application of suncream on a scorching summer day on his bare top. As the game unfolded Rasher was beginning to get very distressed and his performance fell well below his normal standards. During half-time in consultation with the physio it emerged that a tragic mistake had been made. It was not sun cream he had applied on his bald patch but deep heat! Undaunted, the Rasher put his head under the shower and in the second half went out to have the game of his life, scoring a stunning 2–4.

ASHES TO ASHES

The glory years of Roscommon football came in the 1940s. Jimmy Murray's pub-cum-grocery in Knockcroghery is arguably the spiritual home of Roscommon football, with all its memorabilia from the county's only All-Ireland successes in 1943 and 1944, both under the captaincy of Jimmy Murray, including the football from the 1944 final. The football survived a close shave some years ago when Jimmy's premises were burned down – as he recalled to me with mixed feelings:

> The ball was hanging from the ceiling and of course the fire burned the strings and the ball fell down and rolled safely under the counter. The fire happened on a Saturday night and when the fire brigade came one of the firemen jumped off and asked Jimmy, 'Is the ball safe?' As I was watching my business go up in smoke the ball wasn't my main priority! But the fireman came out later with the ball intact. The next day I got calls from all over the country asking if the ball was safe. I was a bit annoyed at the time that all people seemed to be concerned with was the safety of the ball and nobody seemed to be too bothered about what happened to the shop.

CAPTAIN SENSIBLE

Kevin McStay describes the late Jimmy Murray as 'the father of Roscommon football, Jimmy's son John describes his father as a GAA Catholic: 'He went to one Mass on a Sunday and two matches!'

When he got his first football, though, the omens for Jimmy did not suggest that such a glittering career lay ahead of him:

> Santa brought it to me. I spent all of Christmas Day and Stephen's Day kicking it with my neighbours. To preserve its grandeur I thought I should grease it with neatsfoot oil, which farmers used to soften leather boots. When I had it greased, I left it, in my innocence, in front of a big open fire to dry. After a few minutes there was a loud explosion and the ball was in bits. Happily Santa came back again two nights later with a new and better ball.

THE LYNCH MOB

Brendan Lynch was one of four Roscommon players to be selected on the Connacht Team of the Millennium. Lynch came into national prominence when he established the right half-back position as his own and would announce his arrival on the national stage in bold print in the All-Ireland semi-final against Louth in 1943:

> I was marking Peter Corr who had been the player of the year at that stage. He had scored thirteen points in the Leinster final. I decided it was his career or mine. I handled him roughly and kept him scoreless. Peter, who was related to the singers the Corrs, went on to play for Everton. Years later I had moved to the Gardaí and was on traffic duty and a man asked me: 'Are you the fella who terrorised Peter Corr?'
>
> My lasting memory from the game was when the County Secretary, John Joe Fahy, came running up to me at the end of

the game and said, 'Ye'll beat them in the second half if you play like that.' I turned to him and said, 'We have already.' He looked shocked and said, 'God did I miss it.' He was so embroiled in the whole game and the tension it created he had lost all track of time.

Roscommon lost to Cavan in the All-Ireland semi-final in 1947. As Roscommon's fortunes faded Lynch found himself, in a fit of desperation by the selectors, playing at full-forward. From his point of view the initial experiment worked disastrously well as he scored two goals and was kept in the purgatory of the full-forward position for longer than he wished: 'I found out that full-backs are really kicking jennets. A full-forward needs to be an animal.'

ALL IN THE GAME

Roscommon went outside the county borders to get training expertise from former Galway great Tom Kelly. Tom explained to Brendan Lynch his philosophy of the game with an incident from his days in the maroon and white:

Tom told me that he was marking the great Larry Stanley of Kildare, one of the most skillful players in the history of the game. Tom knew the only chance he had with Larry was to rough him up. The first ball that came in between them, Tom caught Stanley on the back of his leg with the nails of his boot. He ripped through not only one of Stanley's socks but a good chunk of his skin as well. Stanley shouted at him: 'That's not how you play football.'

Kelly looked him straight in the eye with all the malice he could master and said: 'Maybe not but that's how I play it.'

Born to Run

One of the fittest men on the team that won the All-Ireland in 1944 was John Joe Nerney. When he was seventy-two years of age John Joe was doing laps of the pitch in Boyle. He saw a thirteen-year-old and decided to challenge him to a race from the half-way line to the goals. The young lad won the race by ten yards. John Joe said: 'The best of three.' John Joe won the next two.

An Act of Treason

The 2012 Connacht club final had a unique pairing when two Roscommon teams, St Brigid's and Ballaghaderreen, contested. For historical reasons Ballaghaderreen take part in the Mayo championship. Roscommon fans have not always appreciated this fact when Ballaghaderreen players go on to play for Mayo despite the fact that they were born in Roscommon. During the 2011 Connacht final, played in almost arctic conditions in the Hyde, whenever Mayo's All-Star forward Andy Moran touched the ball a lone voice was heard to boom out: 'Traitor, Traitor, Traitor.'

Bloody Hell

As this chapter closes we return again to Shane Curran. In 2003 Roscommon played Galway in the Connacht championship. Before the match Curran was in full Russell Crowe in *Gladiator* mode and intent on whipping the Rossies into a frenzy. He urged the team to give every last drop of blood to the cause. He stunned his teammates though by throwing a bag of blood on the dressing room floor to stress the point. He told them that he had got the team doctor, Martin Daly, to take a pint of his blood to highlight the lengths he was prepared to go for the team. To this day the Roscommon players are unsure if it actually was his own blood – but knowing him they think he might just have been crazy enough to do it!

That was not the end to his stunts. He brought two pairs of gloves with him and put on the old pair and absolutely layered it with Vaseline. Before the match he ran up to the Galway goalkeeper Alan Keane to shake hands with him hoping to cover his hands in Vaseline so that he would let in a soft goal as a result. Keane shook his hand and Curran smiled with relish at this prospect on his way back to change into his new gloves but sadly for him the Galway netminder Keane had the sense and sensibility to cop on to his tricks before the Vaseline did any damage and changed his gloves also.

And how was Curran rewarded for his cunning and unique motivational style? … Galway hammered Roscommon!

INSULTING REQUEST

Roscommon did not begin 2014 positively for their manager John Evans, losing the FBD League final to Leitrim. Evans first came to prominence as trainer of leading Carlow club team Éire Óg. He famously said that there were some of his team that he wouldn't insult by sending them to a sports psychologist and others he wouldn't insult the sporting psychologist by sending them to him!

CHAPTER SEVENTEEN

The Flair Factor

Some sports stars are known for their clever comments. A case in point is Brian O'Driscoll who said: 'Knowledge is knowing that a tomato is a fruit. Wisdom is knowing not to put it in a fruit salad.' Down through the years many gaelic footballers have added to the gaiety of the nation with their comments and their antics on and off the pitch. This chapter celebrates some of them.

NOTHING BUT THE TRUTH

Former Laois star Colm Parkinson was being interviewed on Newstalk radio and remarked that whenever there was a controversy it was always branded a 'scandal' in the county. The interviewer, Ger Gilroy, asked: 'Why is that?'

Parkinson calmly replied: 'Probably because we were always drinking.'

Parkinson was also characteristically candid when asked for an evaluation of his own performance for Ireland against Australia in the Compromise Rules series; he had been marking a player who had a big physical advantage over him: 'The first time I tried to tackle this big fella I was holding on to his jersey and he started to run down the pitch. I don't think he even noticed I was holding on to him.'

RUNAROUND SUE

Laois have produced many football greats like Tommy 'The Boy Wonder' Murphy; Tom Kelly; Ross Munnelly and Sue Ramsbottom. With Mayo's Cora Staunton and Cork's Juliet Murphy, Sue is recognised as one of the greats of the modern game. She has gone boldly where no female has gone before. She won her Laois under-12 county championship medal playing with the parish boys' team.

The teenage years are notorious for their fads, prompting many a frustrated parent to say, usually more in hope than in confidence, 'It's just a phase they're going through.' When most of her contemporaries were besotted with the fresh faces of Jason Donovan and Bros (there were many who said the band should have been called Dross) Sue's two heroes were less likely pin-up material – Barney Rock and Colm O'Rourke!

EQUAL OPPORTUNITIES

Sue Ramsbottom is a natural athlete. Apart from winning All-Ireland medals in basketball, volleyball and of course in ladies football she is also an international rugby player. She has an eye for a challenge: 'Give me some mens county team and I'd get them into shape. There'd be some shock wouldn't there? Pat Spillane would have something to say then!'

AFTERNOON TEA

Sue witnessed some unusual sights in the dressing room. Laois were losing at half-time and when they got back to the dressing room one of their mentors said, 'I've put the kettle on and we'll have a cup of tea.' Their manager immediately thumped the table ferociously and everything on it went flying all over the place. Then he yelled (in less polite language), 'How the hell could you think of tea at a time like this?'

LULU

Sue's great friend was her teammate and former co-star with Laois, Lulu Carroll, whose short life was ended so tragically after illness. It was her persistence and nagging of her teacher, Mr Sayers, that led the way for girls to play on a boys national schools team. Lulu got a great kick out of saving penalties on the boys and would taunt them with: 'Ah you couldn't score a goal on a girl.'

Lulu played in the forwards, midfield, backs and goals. Many people have done this before and many will do this in the future but the difference is, Lulu was brilliant in all these positions with All-Stars and replacement All-Stars to prove it. The year 1996 in particular was a great year for Lulu with the sports commentators calling her 'the Liam McHale of ladies football with her long tanned legs'.

FREE THE LAOIS ONE

Lulu was responsible for a song that got a lot of media attention. For one of their All-Ireland finals the Laois team had painted a Beetle in the Laois colours, blue and white, put all their names on it, and parked the car as near as possible to Croke Park on the day of the match. The next morning, they heard the car was missing. It had been impounded because there was no tax on it – the car was so old there was no point in paying tax on it for the day, though it was insured. The team were staying in a hotel in Lucan but they decided to go into the city centre to rally outside the police station and try and get the car back. The sight of all the women singing outside the cop shop created a media sensation and was discussed on Marian Finucane's radio show before a professor from Trinity College volunteered to pay the £100 fine and the car was released.

Lulu's lyrics were:

Where's the Beetle gone?
Far, far way. The cops took it away.

BENCHWARMING

At a time when Meath and Dublin were drawing more often than Don Conroy, Colm O'Rourke was voted footballer of the year. O'Rourke won two All-Ireland medals, three League titles and three All-Stars. However, what he will probably be best remembered for is his part in the four game saga which enthralled the nation in the first round of the Leinster championship in 1991. At a time when Ireland was going through soccer mania after Italia '90 and when the nation was under the spell of Jack Charlton, the series of games proved reports of the GAA's demise to be premature.

Despite their intensity the four game saga did produce one moment of light relief. Paul Curran was dropped for the third game but came on in the second half and scored the equalising point. A few nights later Dublin manager Paddy Cullen had a team meeting with the players and did some video analysis with them. Cullen was severely critical of the forwards first-half performance and turned to Curran and asked him: 'Where were you in the first half?'

To the hilarity of his teammates Curran replied: 'Sitting beside you, as a sub on the bench Paddy!'

MIGHTY MEATH

In the 1970s Dublin's great rivals were Kerry but in the late 1980s and 1990s their most intense rivalry was with Meath. In 1983 after Dublin won the All-Ireland they travelled to Navan for the opening round of the National League. The All-Ireland champions were welcomed onto the field by the Meath team lining either side of the dugout. While the team applauded the Dubs, a Meath player was caught by one photographer giving the champs the two fingers!

HERE'S TO YOU MRS ROBINSON

During her seven years as Irish President Mary Robinson had many visits to Croke Park. Such was the strict protocol, there was very little danger of a surprise for her. But things do not always go to plan. In the strain of an All-Ireland final in 1996 against Mayo Colm Coyle reduced his teammates to laughter when he asked President Robinson as she was being introduced to the Meath team before the match, with the familiarity of intimacy, 'How are things at home?'

BARR-ED

The rivalry between fans can be nasty or it can be witty. When Dublin played Meath in the 1996 Leinster final Meath's Tommy Dowd was in a clash of heads with Dublin's Keith Barr. Some time later Keith's brother, Johnny, was also in the wars with Tommy. After the match Tommy was going up for an interview when he banged his head against a bar on one of the barriers – an injury which subsequently necessitated four stitches. As he held his head in agony a passing Dublin fan said to him, 'I see you made the hat-trick.'

'What do you mean?' Tommy asked.

'Johnny Barr, Keith Barr and Iron Bar!'

SQUARE BALL

During a Dublin–Meath game in the 1990s the Dub fans were giving the Meath goalie, Mickey McQuillan a bit of stick. A few started throwing coins at him. Mickey collected the coins, discovered he had fifty pence and he went over to the umpires and presented him with the money and said, 'There you are now. Any square ball that comes in, you know what to do! Put the money towards a pint.'

LETS GET PHYSICAL

In 1996 after the All-Ireland semi-final two irate Tyrone fans were loud in their condemnation of the Meath team, particularly of their alleged ill-treatment of Peter Canavan. A Meath fan made an interesting and revealing slip of the tongue in response, 'You can't make an omelette without breaking a few legs.'

GARDA REPORT

The face of Meath football was changed forever with the appointment of the great Seán Boylan as Meath manager in 1982. Shortly after he became manager, Dublin were playing Meath in Croke Park. Seán wanted to make a positional change during the match and walked down along the sideline behind the goal in front of the Hill. All the Dublin fans were jeering him and slagging him. Because he was so new in the job and Meath weren't having huge success at the time a garda came racing up to him and thought he was just a fan! Boylan had a fierce problem convincing him that he was actually the Meath manager. After a lot of cajoling Boylan eventually persuaded him of his identity and he said to him, 'You do your job and look after the spectators and let me do my job and look after these lads on the pitch.' After they had finished their 'chat' Boylan walked back in front of the Hill again. This time the Dublin fans gave him a great ovation. They thought he was a hero because he had stood up to and had a big row with a guard!

HELL AND BACK

Under Boylan's stewardship Meath carved out a reputation for never being beaten until the final whistle sounded. Hence, Martin Carney's evaluation of Boylan's boys, 'Meath are like Dracula. They're never dead till there's a stake through their heart.'

After their clashes with Cork in 1987 and 1988 in particular Meath got the reputation of being hard men. Seán Boylan attended a funeral in 1989 and met a young recruit to the Meath panel who took the wind out of the manager's sails by claiming, 'When I die I want to go to hell.'

A bemused Boylan asked, 'Why do you want to go down there?'

'Well now that I'm on the panel I want to be one of the lads in every way. If all the things that are said about them are true the only possible place they could end up is roasting in the fires of the hell!'

Muscular Meath

The popular perception of Meath football is probably best captured in the following quotes:

The rules of Meath football are basically simple – if it moves, kick it; if it doesn't move, kick it until it does.

Tyrone fan after controversial All-Ireland semi-final in 1996.

Meath make football a colourful game – you get all black and blue.

Cork fan in 1987.

Meath players like to get their retaliation in first.

Cork fan in 1988.

Lady of Red

In a previous generation one of the great characters in Meath football was Patsy (Red) Collier. In the 1960s he took part in the Cardinal Cushing Games in America. Some of the players were walking down the street in Washington one day and they passed what they thought was just a public house. Red looked in and called them back and said, 'Jaysus, come back here lads. Ye never saw anything like this.' The players went back to see what he was so excited about. There was a woman up on the bar doing a strip-tease.

WESTMEATH BACHELORS

One of Red's colleagues on that trip was Westmeath's Mick Carley. The most memorable incident of Carley's career came when he was marking Seán Heavin, who he played with for Westmeath, in a club match. Mick was playing centre-forward and he was at the end of his career so his legs were going. At one stage the ball came in to Mick and Seán and was about ten foot in the air. Seán was younger and much quicker than Mick so he had Carley beat; however, just as Seán was about to jump and claim the ball Mick let a roar, 'Let it go Seán.' Heavin stopped and let down his hands and the ball fell into Mick's arms. The whole field opened up for him and he just ran through and tapped it over the bar.

OFFALY ROVERS

Mick once played a club match in Offaly against Walsh Island. After the game was over he changed and was about to go home when a fella called him over and told him he should stay for a junior match between Clonbullogue and Bracknagh. Mick did not really want to but the man was adamant that he should stay. Mick agreed to stay for five minutes. There was nothing special for the first couple of minutes but then suddenly a fracas developed and all hell broke loose. Every one was swinging and punching. Mick found out later that they were all intermarried and there was a lot of history there. It took about five minutes for the referee to sort things out and get order back. He send one of the lads off but the player in question did not do the usual thing, which would be to go back to the dressing room and take a shower. Instead he stood on the sideline waiting for things to boil over again so he could get back into the thick of the fighting. He did not have long to wait. Another melee broke out and they went at it again, only twice as hard this time. The referee finally restored order. But almost as soon as he threw the ball back in another scrap broke out. There was no more than five minutes of football in the first half. In fact things were so bad that at half-time the priests from the two parishes went in to try and calm things down.

Things then got really bad in the second half!

A BROAD CANVAS

Footballers have often been the stimulus for a wide range of reflections on a variety of topics such as:

Football and sex are so utterly different. One involves sensuality, passion, emotion, commitment, selflessness, the speechless admiration of sheer heart-stopping beauty, rushes of breathtaking, ecstatic excitement, followed by shattering, toe-curling, orgasmic pleasure. And the other is sex.

Joe O'Connor.

The whole point about death, metaphorically speaking, is that it is almost bound to occur before the major trophies have been awarded.

Kerry fan.

Last guys don't finish nice.

Frustrated Leitrim fan.

Why did they not take off their pyjamas?
A young boy to his father in 1960
watching Down became the
first inter-county team to wear tracksuits.

In terms of the Richter scale, this defeat was a force eight gale.
Meath fan after the 2001 All-Ireland final.

The grub in the hotel was the only good thing about the day.
Nemo Rangers fan after the 2002 All-Ireland club final.

It gives a whole new meaning to 'powder your nose'.
*Fans reaction to a rumour that a player
was reacting to pressure by taking cocaine.*

The GAA is an amateur association run by professionals. The FAI is a professional body run by amateurs.
Fan during the Roy Keane World Cup saga.

THE LONGFORD LEADER

Jimmy Flynn was literally at the centre of the most successful period of Longford's history. His towering performances at midfield helped the county to beat the mighty Galway in the National League final in 1966. In 1968 Flynn helped Longford to take their only Leinster senior title. The most formative influence on his career was one of the most famous characters in the history of Longford football, Bertie Allen. As a boy, Jimmy played a nine-a-side juvenile match in Longford. Jimmy's side were winning a lot of ball and sending it in to the forwards but they couldn't score. At half-time Bertie said that the four forwards were like Khrushchev, Eisenhower, Macmillan and de Gaulle they were so far apart.

THE LIFE OF O'REILLY

Wicklow have always produced great footballers, though never enough at the one time. Among their greatest was Gerry O'Reilly in the 1950s. His favourite character in the game was Kit Carroll from Dunlavin who played with him on the Wicklow minor team. Like Gerry he was fond of a pint after a game. What was unusual about Kit though was that after a match he would have an auction at the bar for his socks and jersey and would always get a pound or two to fund his drinking.

Gerry attributes the failure of the Wicklow team of the 1950s to the inadequacies of the County Board. He claims that the men on the County Board were so incompetent they couldn't even pick their own noses.

Simply the Best

Like Tyrone's Iggy Jones and so many players from the West of Ireland, Sligo's Micheál Kearins missed out on an All-Ireland medal. Micheál Ó Muircheartaigh furnished the definitive epitaph to Kearins's career, 'Some players are consistent. Some players are brilliant but Micheál Kearins was consistently brilliant.'

His first Railway Cup game was against Leinster in Ballinasloe. At the start, as he was moving into position before the ball was thrown in, he noticed his immediate opponent, Paddy McCormack digging a hole along the ground with his boot.

He said, 'You're young Kearins, from Sligo. I presume you expect to go back to Sligo this evening?'

'Hopefully,' Kearins replied.

'If you don't pass the mark, you have a fair chance of getting back.'

Barnes Murphy gives a different context to that story:

A lot of people know the story of Micheál Kearins' first game with Connacht, marking Paddy McCormack. What they don't know is the postscript. Mickey was switched off Paddy and Cyril Dunne went on his place. Cyril went up to Paddy and said immediately: 'Watch yourself or I'll give you a box.' Paddy was very quiet for the rest of the game.

POLITE CONVERSATION

After a glittering career with Sligo, Kearins became a referee. As a referee he is probably best remembered for two games. In one he controversially sent Meath star Colm O'Rourke off. The other was an All-Ireland semi-final between Cork and Dublin in 1989. He had to send Keith Barr off that day. Having been involved in an incident five minutes earlier, Barr ran thirty yards to get involved in a second. There was an awful lot of off-the-ball stuff that day and it's very hard to manage those games. In fact the tension escalated to such an extent that Kearins publicly pulled the captains, Dinny Allen and Gerry Hargan, aside before the start of the second half and instructed them to warn their players about their behaviour. He didn't get exactly the response he hoped for from Allen who, when quizzed by the Cork lads about what the referee said, claimed Kearins had simply wished them well for the second half and hoped the awful weather would improve.

BRILLIANT BARNES

In 1974 Roscommon needed a replay to beat Sligo in a National League semi-final. Sligo's Barnes Murphy was rewarded for a string of fine performances through the year with an All-Star award. There is one Sligo player though who is most associated with Murphy.

> Micheál Kearins had a serious side and a funny side. We were travelling to a match one day and Micheál, unusually, was coming on the team bus with us. It was often said that Sligo were a one-man team. Someone asked Micheál how the team were going. He replied: 'I'm feeling great today!'
> In 2008 Micheál had a confrontation with a bull and the bull won. Micheál has put on a bit of weight since his playing days and when a friend of mine heard the news he rang me to inquire if the bull was okay!

GLAMOUR

The fact that forwards have featured so prominently in this chapter indicates that they are in the glamour position in gaelic football. Accordingly, they have been the source and subject of a number of humorous quotations including:

Somebody should check his birth cert because I don't think he was born, I think he's a creation of God.

Colm O'Rourke on the apparently divine Colm 'Gooch' Cooper.

I used to think it was great being a wee nippy corner-forward, but it's better now being a big, burly one.

Ollie Murphy.

Mayo always had a big problem coping with being favourites and never lost it!

Former Mayo star, Willie McGee.

They said we were like the British Army, that we lose our power when we cross the border, but we've proved we have power today.

Peter Canavan as he lifted the Sam Maguire Cup.

Those guys are going to be bleeding all over us.

*Cork player responds to the sight
of a very heavily bandaged Willie Joe Padden
in the 1989 All-Ireland final.*

Jaysus, if Lee Harvey Oswald was from Mayo, JFK would still be alive.

Frustrated Mayo fan on the shortcomings of their forwards.

Even Iarnród Éireann don't carry as many passengers as we saw today.

Colm O'Rourke's verdict on the
Dublin and Offaly forwards in the 2007 Leinster semi-final.

If Dublin win, it's overhyped; if Dublin lose, it's overhyped.
Ciarán Whelan.

He'll regret this to his dying day, if he lives that long.
Dub fan after Charlie Redmond missed a penalty
in the 1994 All-Ireland final.

He [Colin Corkery] is as useless as a back pocket in a vest.
Kerry fan.

Colin Corkery is deceptive. He's slower than he looks.
Kerry fan.

INTERNATIONAL ATTRACTION

Sligo's most famous player in the modern era is Eamonn O'Hara. His appeal is international: 'I got a text from a friend on holiday in Portugal. He was surprised to see a Portuguese boy approaching wearing a Sligo jersey. When the boy turned around the saw the number eight on his back with the word O'Hara!'

SUN CONFUSION

Although at the time it was not funny O'Hara now laughs at a case of mistaken identity:

> We were playing Westmeath in 2006. I was given a second yellow card for a foul even though I was forty yards away at the time. The linesman fingered me because he mistook me for Seán Davey because we have the same colour. I'm naturally like this. Seán gets his colouring from a sunbed.

Competition

Like their attacking counterparts, defences have also been the cause of many a funny quote including:

They didn't drink like a fish. They drank like a shoal of mackerel.
Awestruck fan marvels at the drinking powers
of the great Kerry team of the 1970s.

That's the first time I've seen anybody limping off with a sore finger!
Armagh's Gene Morgan to 'injured' teammate Pat Campbell.

Journalist: How's the leg Kevin?
Kevin Moran: It's very fuc … it's very sore.

Francie Bellew marked so tight he would follow opponents to the dressing room at half-time.
Martin McHugh.

I don't want to sit on the fence, but this game could go either way.
Paul Curran.

Graham Geraghty may not be sugar but he adds plenty of spice.
Meath fan.

Superquinn

Mickey Quinn was Leitrim's first All-Star. He admits to playing a leading role in the infamous 'battle of the fog':

Aughawillian were playing Clann na Gael in the Connacht club championship but the match shouldn't have gone ahead. The fog was so bad you couldn't see the goalie kicking out the ball. Things heated up when two of our players were hit. I think it was me who really started it off! I 'had a go' at Jimmy McManus and soon the whole set of players, subs and supporters were involved. The referee had a hard time getting law and order back but the game was a great battle in every sense.

The match did have an amusing postscript though:

Jerome Quinn played for Aughawillian that day and really dished it out to some of the Clann lads and developed a reputation as a hard nut. That was one of the reasons why Aughawillian versus Clann was renamed 'the Provos versus the Guards'. We were playing Roscommon in the Connacht championship in 1990 and before the match PJ Carroll had an unusual mind game planned. He said: 'Jerome Quinn, they all think your f**king mad in Roscommon, what you need to do is pick up a clump of grass, stick it in your mouth and eat it in front of your marker's face. He'll sh*t himself.' Jerome was wing half-back and was marking a lovely, skillful player. Sure enough Jerome did as he was told and you could see the Roscommon player's legs turn to jelly!

SCAPEGOAT

Of course, Leitrim's most legendary footballer is Packy McGarty. He once told me about one of his first club games as a minor. At that stage it was hard to field a team. There was one guy roped in to play for them and he was provided with boots, socks and a jersey. They were thrashed and of course when that happens everybody blames everybody else. When unflattering comments were put to the new recruit, his riposte was, 'Well you can't blame me. I never got near the ball!'

THE BITTER WORD

A Leitrim football fan was shouting abuse at one of their corner-backs: 'Take that useless c**t off, he's good for nothing.'

Another fan intervened: 'That's terribly insulting. Imagine if he was your son.'

The first came back with an unexpected response: 'That useless f**ker is my son!'

CAPTAIN FANTASTIC

One of gaelic football's great gentlemen was Dermot O'Brien. He captained Louth to their only senior All-Ireland title in 1957 but he had more fame as a singer and smashed records with his biggest hit *The Merry Ploughboy*.

One of Dermot's favourite stories was about the Louth player of the 1950s who on a visit to America was chatted up by a woman in a bar. To put it very charitably she was less than pretty and was as heavy as the two Louth midfielders combined. At first the Louth player was immune to the woman's charms. His attention though was captured when she told him that her mother had only two months to live and the dying widow had inherited a multimillion dollar fortune from her husband. Now the daughter stood to inherit everything. The Louth player was moved to action.

Two weeks later he was married … to the mother.

FERGIE TIME

Alex Ferguson style mind games are now in vogue in the GAA. Former Donegal selector Rory Gallagher aired his conspiracy theory before their 2013 All-Ireland quarter-final meeting with Mayo: 'We suspect there was a bit of collusion between Monaghan and Mayo. [James] Horan works to a premediated script and I think Kieran Shannon is behind a good bit of it.'

Newstalk's Colm Parkinson immediately described it as 'Mind James'.

ALL IN THE NAME GAME

Colm Parkinson of Newstalk went on to describe his own mind games. He would shake hands with his opponent before a big match and call them deliberately the wrong name just to throw them off their game for a few minutes at least.

THE FOREIGN GAME

Sporting ecumenism is alive and well in the GAA, as is evident from the keen analysis some of our top personalities paid to the 2014 World Cup. After Germany beat Brazil 7–1 Monaghan's Dick Clerkin tweeted: 'If David Luiz was a house he would be a 3 Bed semi in Longford bought in 2007 #negative_equity'

Robin van Persie's less than stellar performance in the semi-final prompted Eamonn O'Hara's barb: 'Van Persie playin[g] much better since he was taken off.'

Cavan's Michael Hannon saw the funny side of George Hamilton's commentary in the penalty shoot-out in that same game: '"the awful realisation has dawned on these [Dutch] players, Its down to Dirk Kuyt." Classic George Hamilton penalty commentary #rteworldcup'

Paul Galvin, though, came up with this priceless observation: 'Sickened #Klose beat the great Ronaldo's record. That's not right. The last time Klose dribbled past a man he was about to vomit in the mens.'

GETTING YOUR TEETH INTO IT

The classic comment on the World Cup came from Gort when Cooles under-tens played the Burren. A very quick-witted eight year old, Harry Minogue, spotting a hole in his jersey remarked, 'Look lads, Suarez must be in town.'

RECIPROCITY

For their part, soccer stars have been won over to hurling thanks to Sky Sports. Witness Joey Barton's tweet after Tipperary's demolition of Cork in the 2014 All-Ireland semi-final: 'These hurling fella don't even wear gloves. Fingers like steel... #somegame'

CHAPTER EIGHTEEN

Shiny, Unhappy People

In its long history fans have provided the GAA with a motley crew of interesting individuals who have created some moments of mischief, mirth and mayhem. This chapter pays homage to some of their more memorable moments.

FANS FORUM

Of course the GAA has attracted its share of famous fans. Eamon de Valera attended every All-Ireland final during his presidency – even though by the end of his reign he was almost totally blind. One of his latter-day All-Irelands had a number of controversial refereeing decisions. The losing manager was asked for his thoughts afterwards. He observed: 'Dev saw more of the game than the ref did.'

THE WICKLOW WAY

Tommy Docherty once remarked: 'After the match an official asked for two of my players to take a dope test. I offered him a referee.' It sums up the lack of esteem most people have for referees. In Wicklow though they take things to a whole different level.

Club football in Wicklow is not for the faint-hearted, especially not faint-hearted referees. One of the most famous incidents was when a group of disaffected fans, after losing a club match, locked a referee in the boot of his car. In the return fixture the nervous referee, brought the two teams together and pointed to his whistle and said, 'Do ye see this yoke lads? I'm going to blow it now and blow it again at the finish and whatever happens in between ye can sort out yerselves.'

EYESORE

A referee's lot is not a happy one; it is the only occupation where a man has to be perfect on the first day of the job and then improve over the years. One spectator at a club match in Wicklow was complaining bitterly all through the game about the referee's poor eyesight. At one stage the fan, getting increasingly frustrated, shouted, 'Ah ref, where are your testicles?'

AH REF!

It may have been that knowledge of the GAA scene in Wicklow is what inspired Henry Winter to observe: 'Modern referees need the wisdom of Solomon, the patience of Job, the probity of Caesar's wife, the stamina of Mo Farah and the acceleration of Usain Bolt. Oh, and the thick skin of a rhino.'

BLOOD BOILERS

As countless phone-in shows have demonstrated few things excite the indignation of GAA fans more than referees:

He [the referee] wouldn't see a foul in a henhouse.
                    Frustrated Sligo fan after the 2002 Connacht final.

There are two things in Ireland that would drive you to drink. GAA referees would drive you to drink and the price of drink would drive you to drink.

Another Sligo fan after the same match.

IN THE BEGINNING

Gaelic football was always about more than sport in rural Ireland and in Kerry in particular. Some things never change. From time immemorial football fans have been complaining about referees. In fact a recent archaeological find in Kerry uncovered ancient scrolls of a series of conversations between a caveman from Tralee and his wife. At one point the caveman said: 'I'm still annoyed about watching that match today. The referee was a w*nker.'

In frustration his wife shouted at him: 'Will you ever get off your arse and do something productive like discover fire.'

ALL OR NOTHING

Wicklow fans often use the analogy of bacon and eggs to describe the difference between involvement and commitment in the GAA: the hen is involved in the process through laying the egg but the pig is totally committed!

LOVELY LEITRIM

Another man concerned about warped priorities was a gentleman of the cloth at an emergency meeting of a club in Leitrim: sixty players had gone on a weekend tour of Amsterdam for a sevens tournament, which they were ignominiously dumped out of in the first round, but only a week after they had failed to drum up fifteen players to play Carrick-on-Shannon, just twenty miles down the road. A member of the touring party to Amsterdam responded to the priest's criticism, 'Well father, to the best of my knowledge, there are no ladies of the night in Carrick-on-Shannon.'

OLD RIVALS

One of the best sources of comedy among GAA fans is the intensity of the feeling between rival fans. A case in point goes back to the 1980s and early nineties when Kilkenny's dominance ensured a bleak time for Wexford hurling. This manifested itself in graffiti on the Wexford side of the New Ross bridge, which separates counties Kilkenny and Wexford; a sign there had originally read 'You are now entering a Nuclear Free Zone', but the Kilkenny fans added a note of their own saying 'You've now entered a Trophy Free Zone'.

In 1996 Liam Griffin led Wexford to All-Ireland victory. Some Kilkenny fans could not handle the new hurling order. That Christmas a Kilkenny family went into Callan to do some Christmas shopping. In the sports shop the son picked up a Wexford hurling shirt and said to his twin sister, 'I've decided to be a Wexford supporter and I would like this jersey for Christmas.' His sister, outraged by the suggestion, slapped him on the face and said, 'Go talk to your mother.' The boy walked with the Wexford shirt in hand and found his mother, 'Mummy dearest?'

'Yes pet?'

'I've decided I'm going to be a Wexford supporter and I'd like this shirt for Christmas.'

The mother could barely speak with anger but eventually said, 'Go talk to your father.'

Off he went with shirt in hand and found his father, 'Dad?'

'Yes son.'

'I've decided to become a Wexford supporter and I would like this shirt for Christmas.'

The father hit the son a thump on the head and said, 'No son of mine will be seen in a yoke like that.'

As they went home the father asked the son if he had learned any lesson that day. The son thought for a moment before replying, 'Yes I have. I've only been a Wexford fan for over an hour and already I hate you Kilkenny f**kers!'

THEM AND US

Not surprisingly the intensity of feeling between rival fans has spawned some memorable comments. Among them are the following:

Winning the All-Ireland without beating Cork or Kilkenny is an empty experience, but as empty experiences go it's one of the best.

Tipperary fan in 2001.

A Kildare supporters helpline has been opened. The number is 1800 1 nothing, 1 nothing, 1 nothing.

Meath fan after beating Kildare
in the 2007 Leinster championship.

The Down forward line couldn't strike a match.

Donegal fan after their win
in the Ulster championship in 2002.

To call Donegal lucky would be to call the Atlantic Ocean wet.

Armagh fan after losing to Donegal
because of a late, late 'lucky' goal in 2007.

It's not a North–South thing, sure we're all the same – it's six of one and twenty-six of the others.

Tyrone comic Kevin McAleer
before the 2003 All-Ireland final.

Avoid excitement – watch the Dubs.

Louth fan.

The only suitable replacement for Tommy Lyons that can live up to the aspirations of Dublin fans is Merlin the Magician.

Meath supporter.

I think Mickey Whelan [Dublin manager in 1996] believes tactics are a new kind of piles on your bum.

Disgruntled Mayo fan.

Our defence was as effective as Joe Jacob's iodine tablets in a nuclear holocaust.

Dublin fan after Clare's demolition job in 2002.

NEIGHBOURS

The Longford–Westmeath rivalry is one of the most keenly contested in football, as was apparent in the 2007 Leinster championship.

An old Longford fan was dying and when it was obvious that he had very little time left the local priest, a Westmeath man, was sent for. After the priest administered the last rites he asked the old man if he had any last wish. He was astounded when the man asked if he could join the Westmeath supporters club. The priest though duly pulled out a membership card for the man and helped him to sign his name for the last time. When the priest left, the man's seven stunned sons crowded around the bed and asked their father why he had made this extraordinary request. With practically his dying breath he said: 'Isn't it better for one of them to die than one of our lads.'

EVERYBODY NEEDS GOOD NEIGHBOURS

Monaghan 'enjoy' a great rivalry on the football field with Cavan and their fans are never slow to invoke the stereotypical image of Cavan people, revealed in stories like the Cavan footballer who gave his wife lipstick for Christmas every year so that at least he could get half of it back.

One story they tell is about the Pope. He had a very, very unusual blood type. The doctors could only find one person in the whole world who had the same blood type, Paddy O'Reilly the Cavan footballer. So Paddy donated a pint of blood and the Pope recovered. As a gesture of goodwill the Pope sent Paddy £20,000. The Pope got ill four times in successive years after that and each time he got a pint of Paddy's blood and each time he sent Paddy £20,000. The sixth time he got Paddy's blood the Pope only sent him a holy medal. Paddy was devastated and rang the Vatican to ask why he got no money this time. The Pope's secretary took the call and answered, 'Well Paddy you have to understand he has a lot of Cavan blood in him at this stage!'

That may be why Monaghan fans say that when the Cavan football team go on a short holiday the hotel put their Gideon Bibles on chains.

THE WINNER TAKES IT ALL

For all their fanaticism defeat and dejection are the inevitable diet of most GAA fans as the championship unfolds each year. Some supporters, though, can still raise a smile on their darkest days when their wounds are still painfully raw:

Kerry would have won if Meath hadn't turned up.
A Kerry fan reflects on the All-Ireland semi-final defeat in 2001.

Behind every Galway player there is another Galway player.
Meath fan at the 2001 All-Ireland final.

The Mayo forward line has ISDN – it still does nothing.
Frustrated Ballina man after the loss to Galway in 2007.

Poor Mayo, with no real method up front, resembled a fire engine hurrying to the wrong fire.
Spectator at the infamous 1993 All-Ireland semi-final against Cork.

The natural state of the Antrim football fan is bitter disappointment.
Antrim fan.

Fermanagh has such a small playing base; half is made up of water and half of the remaining half are Protestants!
Fermanagh fan bemoans the paucity of talent.

Mayo fan at 2006 All-Ireland: If you take the defending out of the equation, we played okay.
Kerry fan: If you take the assassination out of the equation, JFK and Jackie enjoyed that drive from Dallas to the airport.

What Billy Morgan needs most is a Bob the Builder set to help him rebuild his Cork team.
Cork fan after losing to Kerry in 2006.

FAMILY TIES

A young boy's parents were getting divorced. The judge asked him: 'Would you like to live with your father?'
    'No he beats me.'
    'So you would like to live with your mother?'
    'No she beats me.'
    'Well who would you like to live with?'
    'The Kilkenny football team – they can beat nobody!'

LAST WILL AND TESTAMENT

A Clare farmer was making out his will the day after Clare lost to Waterford in the 2007 championship. His solicitor was surprised at one of his clauses: 'To Páidí Ó Sé I leave my clown suit. He will need it if he continues to manage as he has in the past.'

Another Clare fan joked after the match that Páidí was going to a fancy-dress party dressed as a pumpkin, hoping at midnight he would turn into a coach.

GAA RIDDLES

Q. What's the difference between Tommy Walsh and Kylie Minogue?
A. Walsh marks tighter than Kylie's famous hotpants.

Q. What do Mayo footballers have in common with a wonderbra?
A. Lots of support but no cup.

Q. What do you say to a Meath man in Croke Park on All-Ireland final day?
A. Two packets of crisps please.

Q. How many Cavan footballers does it take to change a light bulb?
A. Are you paying with Visa or American Express?

Q. What do Kerry footballers use for contraception?
A. Their personalities.

Q. What's the difference between Paddy Cullen and a turnstile?
A. A turnstile only lets in one at a time.

Q. What's the difference between Paddy Cullen and Cinderella?
A. At least Cinderella got to the ball.

Q. Who were the last two Westmeath men to play midfield in the All-Ireland final?
A. Foster and Allen.

Q. How many intelligent Cork fans does it take to screw a light bulb?
A. Both of them.

Q. What's the difference between God and Pat Spillane?
A. God doesn't think he's Pat Spillane.

SECURITY CONSCIOUS

Before Meath played Dublin in 2007 an anxious Meath fan boldly parked his car at Archbishop's House in Drumcondra. Just when he thought his troubles were over some of the Dublin fans started chanting at him: 'We know where your car is parked do-dah, do-dah.'

THE WEE COUNTY

In 2007 a new rivalry emerged between Louth and Wicklow during the three games they played in the Leinster championship. It would have meant so much to Wicklow football to have put one over on their more illustrious rivals. Sky Sports were asking people leaving the England match after their 1–1 draw to Brazil in Wembley if they were disappointed.

Fan: 'Not at all, I'm Irish, I'm from Bray.'
Reporter: 'But would you not support England when Ireland are not action?'
Fan. 'No way.'

Reporter: 'Why not?'

Fan: 'Eight hundred years of oppression.'

Reporter: 'Is there ever any time you would support England?'

Fan: 'If they were playing Louth.'

MEDICAL MIRACLE

Armagh fans were not happy with the way the Tyrone forwards, especially Brian Dooher, would go to ground after any light physical contact and, perish the thought, might exaggerate the nature of their injuries. They started a rumour that after a particularly theatrical fall Dooher thought he was dead. When the Tyrone team doctor went on to the pitch he found it tough to convince Dooher he was still alive. Nothing seemed to work. Finally the doctor tried one last approach. He took out his medical books and proceeded to show the then Tyrone captain that dead men don't bleed. After a long time Dooher finally seemed convinced that dead men don't bleed.

'Do you now agree that dead men don't bleed?' the doctor asked.

'Yes, I do,' Dooher replied.

'Very well, then,' the doctor said.

He took out a pin and pricked Dooher's finger. Out came a trickle of blood.

The doctor asked, 'What does that tell you?'

'Oh my goodness!' Dooher exclaimed as he started incredulously at his finger. 'Dead men do bleed!'

FANDOM

GAA fans are known for the sharpness of their tongue. The following selection provides the book of evidence:

I was expecting a dictatorship of experts. Instead we have a dictatorship of idiots.

> *Waterford fan on the pundits after beating hotly-fancied Clare*
> *in the 2007 Munster championship.*

John O'Mahony has given up football. He's just become Kildare manager.

> *Galway fan.*

The toughest match I ever heard off was the 1935 All-Ireland semi-final. After six minutes the ball ricocheted off the post and went into the stand. The pulling continued relentlessly and it was twenty-two minutes before any of the players noticed the ball was missing!

> *Michael Smith.*

There is nothing even vaguely intellectual about a Munster hurling final, yet a proper enjoyment of the game presupposes a sophisticated appreciation of the finer things.

> *David Hanly.*

If you put monkeys on to play they'd still pack Croke Park on All-Ireland final day.

> *Kilkenny fan.*

Cork hurling games are like sex films – they relieve frustration and tension.

> *Joe Lynch.*

Why are Limerick magic? Because they can disappear for five minutes.

Offaly hurling final after the dramatic 1994 All-Ireland final.

MINTY FRESH

January 2014 saw yet more allegations about biting during an inter-county match. Suggestions have been made that if the trend continued the GAA could get sponsorship from all the toothpaste companies.

CHAPTER NINETEEN

The Maestro

Micheál Ó Muircheartaigh is one broadcaster who is universally loved. He is completely free from the pretension associated with many of his colleagues. His style is unique. Hence, Jack O'Shea's comment: 'He [Micheál] can take the ball from one end of the field to the other with just the players' occupations.'

Micheál has carved out a unique place in the affections of Irish sport lovers over the last fifty years. The most mundane of matches come alive through his commentary. Everything he says into his microphone is informed by a passion that is as natural to him as breathing. His commentaries are famous for the richness of their texture, abounding with references that delight and surprise. He was born in Dún Síon, near Dingle in Kerry. He paints a picture of an idyllic childhood growing up on his parent's dairy farm. The fourth of eight children, a young Micheál loved riding the horse, bringing the milk to the creamery, and being by the sea.

After qualifying as a teacher he took up a post with the Christian Brothers in a Dublin school. The sad reality is that he would probably not get a job in RTÉ if he was applying now because of his lack of experience. His story is the broadcasting equivalent of *Roy of the Rovers*. He was only eighteen, training to be a teacher and still adjusting to life in Dublin when a friend saw a notice on the college noticeboard for part-time Irish-speaking commentators. The auditions were at Croke Park, a club game was in progress, and each applicant was given a five-minute slot – an opportunity to sort out the real thing from the pretenders:

A group of us went – we went with the idea that it would be great fun, we'd be in Croke Park, a place we revered, and most importantly, we knew we would get in for free. It was an adventure.

They had to pick somebody and they picked me. It is still a very vivid memory. Naturally none of us knew any of the players, but I knew one who went to school in Dingle, Teddy Hurley, and another player in midfield. I just talked away at random and people I knew featured very prominently, even though they were not on the scene of the action at all! I then moved into the big money league and was offered a massive contract – all of £6!

One of Micheál's coups was to become the first person to interview a British Royal, Prince Edward, on RTÉ radio. As joint owner of *Druid's Johnno*, Prince Edward was celebrating his semi-final victory in the English Greyhound Derby at Wimbledon. Micheál stepped up and asked in his velvety soft tones, as only he can, 'Now tell me, Prince.'

Micheál's golden voice is all a GAA devotee needs to ignite their passion, as is revealed in this story: A man and his wife were making love. Suddenly she noticed something sticking in his ear. Not surprisingly, she enquired what it was. He replied, 'Be quiet. I'm listening to the great man.'

Few people have done more to promote the whirr of the flying sliotar and the thrilling sound of ash against ash than the voice from Dingle who makes GAA fans tingle, Micheál. To shamelessly steal from Patrick Kavanagh: 'among his earthiest words the angels stray.'

CLASSIC COMMENTS

Micheál has left an indelible mark on the GAA landscape with a series of classic comments. This is my top baker's dozen of his comments:

1. I see John O'Donnell dispensing water on the sideline. Tipperary, sponsored by a water company. Cork sponsored by a tea company. I wonder will they meet later for afternoon tea.

2. He kicks the ball *lan san aer*, could've been a goal, could've been a point … it went wide.

3. Colin Corkery on the forty-five lets go with the right boot. It's over the bar. This man shouldn't be playing football. He's made an almost Lazarus-like recovery. Lazarus was a great man but he couldn't kick points like Colin Corkery.

4. Stephen Byrne with the puck-out for Offaly … Stephen, one of twelve … all but one are here today. The one that's missing is Mary, she's at home minding the house … and the ball is dropping *í lar na bpairce* …

5. Pat Fox has it on his hurl and is motoring well now … but here comes Joe Rabbitte hot on his tail … I've seen it all now, a rabbit chasing a fox around Croke Park.

6. Pat Fox out to the forty and grabs the sliotar … I bought a dog from his father last week, sprints for goal … the dog ran a great race last Tuesday in Limerick … Fox to the twenty-one, fires a shot, goes left and wide … and the dog lost as well.

7. Danny 'The Yank' Culloty: he came down from the mountains and hasn't he done well.

8. Teddy looks at the ball; the ball looks at Teddy.

9. In the first half they played with the wind. In the second half they played with the ball.

10. 1–5 to 0–8, well from Lapland to the Antarctic, that's level scores in any man's language.

11. I saw a few Sligo people at Mass in Gardiner Street this morning and the omens seem to be good for them, the priest was wearing the same colours as the Sligo jersey! Forty yards out on the Hogan stand side of the field Ciarán Whelan goes on a rampage – it's a goal. So much for religion.

12. And Brian Dooher is down injured. And while he is down I'll tell ye a little story. I was in Times Square in New York last week, and I was missing the championship back home and I said, 'I suppose ye wouldn't have *The Kerryman* would ye?' To which, the Egyptian behind the counter turned to me he said, 'Do you want the North Kerry edition or the South Kerry edition?' He had both, so I bought both. Dooher is back on his feet.

13. David Beggy will be able to fly back to Scotland without an aeroplane he'll be so high after this.